MY TRUTH

MY TRUTH
What Is Yours?

Daniela Szasz

2015

My Truth - What Is Yours? Copyright © 2015 Daniela Szasz

All Rights Reserved. No part of this publication may be reproduced, stored in a retrieval system, or transmitted, in any form or in any means – by electronic, mechanical, photocopying, recording or otherwise – without prior written permission.

The information contained in this book is intended to be educational and not for diagnosis, prescription, or treatment of any health disorder whatsoever. This information should not replace consultation with a competent healthcare professional. The author is in no way liable for any misuse of the material.

Book Cover Design by Beth Hudson

Editing Consultant - Kelly Penman

Book Cover Photos by Grecel Nepomuceno Photography and Daniela Szasz

ISBN 978-0-9940784-0-7

Dedication

This book is dedicated to my daughter Daniela.

Dada,

I am blessed to be your mother. Our Souls knew each other in a past life, the current incarnation making the bond between us even stronger. Your inner beauty always shines. I see you as a strong, creative and wise woman. I am a proud mother.

This is a Thank You gift for choosing me to be your mother, and for the unconditional love you share with me. From my heart to yours. May you always live the truth of your heart and may you always love yourself and everyone unconditionally.

Know my unconditional love for you will always be the Light on your journey.

Blessings always,

Mama

The Meaning Behind My Cover

When the time came to create my cover I knew that I wanted to do it myself, but I had no idea what I wanted my cover to look like. I looked at many books in my home library and checked online, but nothing came to me. One late autumn day as I sat meditating at my favourite place by the lake, with the calm water and warm temperature surrounding me, I looked around and noticed the trees were without leaves. They were ready for their winter rest. I felt like taking some pictures of them.

The clouds moved through the sky and I captured these moments with my camera. Being a digital camera, I immediately looked through the pictures and I knew one of them would be on the cover of my book. I was excited. The first idea for my book cover was born.

Later that autumn, I was at the park again cushion and blanket in hand so that I could meditate. I sat by the water and closed my eyes. I enjoyed the sunshine on my face and the breeze in my hair. Observing my breath, I felt a deep connection to my heart and to my surroundings. I felt the expansion and the connection to Creator; a feeling of oneness.

I allow myself this connection every morning, it is how I consciously choose to start my day—co-creating with the One. I put the intention of what I want to create—out there. This is when I hear Creator speak to me most clearly and strongly. And later that morning, I heard: look up. I opened my eyes and looked towards the sky to see a white cloud shaped like a heart. Beautiful. I photographed it and placed it on the back cover of this book.

The following summer I had several pictures taken, with the plan to choose one for the cover of my book. One of my favourite photos taken that day was the one with the lily. I love flowers and it was my birthday, so holding a flower felt right to me. When the photo shoot was over, I thought how easy, ideas for my book cover were coming together.

When Beth Hudson, my designer, put my cover together for me to see I knew immediately that it had deeper meaning. On the cover, it appeared as though I was looking at the branches. Looking at the cover of my book, my inner voice said the branches of the trees represent dormant life—creative life force energy which always exists within us. We are here to embrace and fully use that energy for our best interests and for the best interests of all. It is how we complete our Soul Mission, the message became clear to me.

As I focused on the lily in the photo, I heard: "Life is always in our hands, we are the creators of our life. Life is beautiful, life is a flower and we are the gardeners." Then I searched the meaning of the red lily, and found a definition that resonated with me. The red lily represents love, ardor, and affection for your loved ones. The lily also symbolizes purity and innocence.

Trust The Wisdom within. If the idea does not come when you want, let go and trust that when the time comes everything will be revealed to you. Know that you are always guided. Believe that when you ask it will be given in perfect Divine Order.

Thank you, Beth, for doing such a wonderful job on my book cover.

Foreword

In her first book, Daniela Szasz presents the fundamental question every spiritual seeker asks at some point: What is my truth?

What is truth? Who decides what is truth? And how do we know what is not true? Ultimately, we—ourselves—decide what is true and come to our own conclusions through experience. The more we penetrate into each experience that life presents the closer we come to discovering universal truths, ultimate truths, higher truths, and the truth of our existence in this vast Universe.

In this book, Daniela offers the reader insight into her own intriguing journey into self-discovery. She shares her hopes, fears, dreams, successes, and failures in a way the reader can empathize with, and use the wisdom she gained for their own benefit.

When reading through the pages one cannot help but feel connected to Daniela, for her struggles are our struggles, despite taking place in different times, with different people, in different lands. Her experience remains universal, as does her quest: to bring oneself closer and closer to love, compassion, contentment, inner peace, and—ultimately—enlightenment.

We are all on the path to enlightenment and our experiences are meant to guide us there. All the good and bad that happen to us are necessary lessons. If we are aware and pay attention to each experience then truth is revealed.

Reading this book itself is a journey. As we read, we become a part of Daniela's journey. If we read with awareness her lessons become our lessons and we can see and feel her growth become our growth as it unfolds, page by page. I encourage you, the reader, to remain deeply aware while reading Daniela's intimate book of her life. She invites you to see through her eyes. She welcomes you into her heart. She offers you encouragement to get through your own difficulties and challenges. Take her hand; let's enjoy the journey together.

With blessings and gratitude,
Johannes Linstead
Multi-award winning Guitarist and Yogi

Acknowledgement

I would like to thank all physical and nonphysical beings who helped bring my book into physical reality.

I am blessed with many amazing friends in my life. All of who helped me with this book for free or very little exchange. I see these people live in state of a higher awareness, where the focus is not on money and business, but rather on help, sharing their gifts and hearts: people who believe in others because they believe in themselves. People who live life with passion and sharing love of the heart and, therefore, believe their monetary needs will always be met.

I am thankful to know you my divine sisters—Stephanie Cicanovski, Michele Hamilton, and Wendy Pitblado. Thank you for your help during the process of writing my book. And a very special thanks to you Maria Benadik for helping proof the final copy.

I want to give special thanks to Kelly—thank you for helping edit my book and for the special friendship we created in a short period of time. I feel I have known you for a long time. I highly value your cooperation, all your good tips, and your happy attitude every time we met to work on editing this book.

I also want to give a special thanks to Lorie Gelsheimer—I appreciate our instant connection when we first met. We share a special bond, a friendship and a knowingness that we were meant to create together in vibrations of divine love.

Most of all I am thankful to my dear family for their support and believing in me. To my daughter, Daniela, who gave me a notebook for Christmas a few years back, which I used to begin this book. To my husband, Attila, who always showed interest in the process and asked how my book was coming along. My love and appreciation for your love is forever in my heart.

I am thankful to all Teachers, Masters, Guides, Angels, Ancestors in the Spirit world who patiently guided me, stood by me, and answered all my questions. Without you guiding me this book would not exist. Last, but not least, I am thankful to my Divine Self for listening to all the guidance provided. I am thankful that I trusted the process, I did not give up, and that I believed I could do it. I am thankful I did.

Introduction

My life shaped me to be the woman I am today. And still does as I am in the process of my life unfolding, like each of us. We are always evolving.

I spent years hearing whispers. These whispers told me to write a book about my life experiences. But I was not ready to write about it, so I put it off. Then one day, I realized the time had come to listen to the voice of my heart. I needed to put my truth into words. Words I felt could serve others on their journey. I wrote what I was guided to write and I knew, for the purposes of this book, that I needed to start the story at the beginning, from when I was born.

I want to share with you Dear Reader, how I became who I am today. It took all those years since I was born and, I believe, many lifetimes before to be the woman I am today. If I could see my life in a movie, I would think this could not be the same person or same lifetime…so many different experiences, living in different countries, speaking different languages, doing different jobs, and experiencing two marriages. A peaceful, loving woman, an unhappy woman, sometimes playful like a child, sometimes serious.

How can that possibly be one person? Yet, it was me. I believe you can relate because it is in all of us. We come to this physical reality to experience a contrast of duality. We come here to learn and to grow, to love, and to feel lack of love sometimes, but only when we choose to. Through all of my experiences I learned to be selective to what I choose to experience. True love is always in our hearts, waiting for us to be seen.

Life is about choices, conscious and, many times, unconscious. We do things automatically, habitually. We come here to explore new territory. Living in a world of duality is the perfect place to live; it allows us to choose what we prefer for ourselves. Our Soul chooses to experience good and bad—as our mind categorizes it. I call our experiences high and low vibrations with everything in-between because everything is energy.

Life feels more meaningful when we choose to see the reality of Source in the world. God, Energy, Creator, Light, however you wish to call the One Source that created our physical world. Source also gave us Free Will to choose what we want to experience in this world. Each of us is free to choose to be a victim or a victor in this life. Those who choose to be a victim will slowly destroy the body with victim belief patterns and behaviors. We are free to be a victor instead, choosing to use the wisdom and strength earned through life's experiences to live any, and all, dreams we dream. Creator loves us, dearly and unconditionally; IT will let us make a choice in our lives. IT will let us suffer or thrive. That is unconditional love.

Part One

Part One

Chapter One

The sixties...

My Soul decided to incarnate again and walk on this beautiful planet Earth, to experience growth through new experiences. My Soul was ready for The Contract.

Two loving, young people in their early twenties met, fell in love, then married, and planned to have a family. They wanted to share the love of their hearts with their children. They would become my parents.

It was a warm evening in June. Maria, now in her mid-twenties and mother of a two-year-old son, Marian, was in labor. It was a quiet evening in a small town in Slovakia, a beautiful countryside at the feet of the Male Karpaty Mountains. It grew darker, the stars and moon hung in a clear sky waiting to welcome a new life, while Maria patiently awaited her husband, Marian, to return from work on the midnight train. Her pain intensified; she knew she must get to the hospital soon. Her husband arrived home and they were off. Everything happened fast. Soon after their arrival, a baby girl was born. Maria held her daughter for the first time, thinking she held the whole world in her arms. It was a joyful moment for the parents to see their baby girl for the first time.

New parents named their daughter Daniela, after Maria's best friend in elementary school. Maria had not seen her school friend since her family moved from the town she had grown-up in. Maria's brother emigrated, and his emigration forced his parents and siblings to move, as they were no longer wanted in their hometown. So Maria named her daughter

Daniela, in remembrance of the long lost friend she once loved to spend time with, not knowing the name meant—God is my judge. She never saw her school friend Daniela again.

My Soul chose my parents to bring me into the physical world to share love and to learn life lessons within this family. I grew up with an older brother, Marian, and a younger sister, Svetlana. My grandmother nicknamed my brother, Berko, after her son (my uncle in Canada) Bernard. We were happy kids. My mother's parents lived with us. My grandparents and my father worked, while my mother stayed home with us. My parents were planning to build a new house. Growing up I felt our family had everything to live a happy life, yet there were challenges. Later in life I understood three generations living together was not always easy. Everyone brings with them different beliefs and hurts from the past.

Now I understand, people hold deep love for each other but sometimes are unable to express it. At times, pain from the past causes us to keep our hearts closed. I understand we all come here to learn different lessons and we learn through our experiences. What is important through the process of our life is to always remember the love.

Chapter Two

I remember going to school...

On a beautiful September morning my mom took me to school for the first time. Dressed in a new pink dress with yellow, blue, and green pastel-colored flowers my mom bought for me for the start grade one, I stood in the schoolyard with many other children. I felt happy. I liked to be with other kids. Everything felt light and bright. I was only six years old but I could feel my independence and a desire to learn and explore. I felt it was going to be an adventure for me to leave home every morning to go to school to meet other kids and teachers.

What I clearly remember now, from those early years of school, was that I never took school seriously. It felt like I went to school to have fun, to play, and to learn only what interested me.

I really liked classes where we created anything with our hands. I loved painting, sewing, woodwork, and helping teachers to organize the classroom. I also liked singing, poetry, writing essays and exercising. And I loved when we were spending time outdoors, running and playing games. I liked geography. I was a dreamer, in these classes, always imagining myself living in a different part of the world. I traveled my childish world in my own mind, even though I was growing up in a communist country where traveling outside the border was for only the fortunate few: those who were in the communist party or in some way privileged. Many times I wondered about life in Canada where my mother's brother had emigrated so long ago. I also liked history, or part of it. I could never understand why we had to learn about wars—people's suffering did not make sense to me. I never concentrated on that, as it never interested me. It did not feel right for me to read about the suffering of humans. I was fascinated when teachers talked about the history of people, different cultures, their lifestyles, their knowledge and creativity. I particularly loved learning about the ancient times of Athens, Greece and the pyramids of Egypt. I always wanted to know more, but they never focused on these topics.

Geometry and biology were subjects I also liked. I liked learning about nature, animals and plants. I was always the first one to help the teacher decorate our classroom for different occasions, such as Christmas. I loved taking care of the plants in the classroom's windows. I loved preparing my costumes for our annual carnival. Those were the things I liked most about my school years.

It makes me smile now, remembering what school meant to me; having fun, creating with my hands and studying subjects I found meaningful. Everything else seemed as though I wouldn't need it. Yes, there was simple math, reading, and writing; these subjects I knew I would need, but they came easy to me and I did not need to study for them. From a young age, I sensed that what I needed to know would come naturally. I never studied very hard through the school years. I never really cared to be one of the best students in the class. Marks were not important to me. I was always an average student and I was happy with it.

My parents never pushed me to study. They had enough on their hands building their house, taking care of their family and the land they owned. They also had a vineyard and a garden to take care of. When I look back to that time of my life, I realize that I was more interested in practical things. I preferred to spend time playing games with the other kids outdoors. I must say that I loved reading books: story books, poetry, the atlas of the world, and books about the Universe, planets and stars. There were few of those when I was growing up. I was fascinated watching the stars and I always wanted to know what was out there.

Besides school, I had many friends. In the long hot days of summer, we played badminton and we rode our bicycles to get ice cream. I always liked the summer. My older brother, his friends, and I would go to the outdoor movie theatre. I especially liked this time of year because I went to camp. Those camps were located in beautiful places in the High Tatras Mountains. We sang on the bus and went on different excursions in the areas. I liked to visit the old castles built centuries before I was born. I often wondered who built the castles and how they did it. I imagined the life of the people who inhabited the buildings many generations before. I was a curious child.

At summer camp, we would sit around the campfire and sing. I enjoyed the warm evenings under the stars, watching the fire and being with a group of happy kids and adults. It was such a fun adventure for me every summer. I did not understand why my siblings did not want to go to summer camp every year. I remember they only went a few times. They preferred to stay at home. My mom did not work when we were growing up. She stayed at home with us so we did not have to go to camp, but I still wanted to go. Many times I felt different than my siblings. I certainly looked different. They had darker skin, dark hair and brown eyes. I was blonde, pale skinned, and blue-eyed. I inherited my blue eyes from my father. Yet still, each year I returned to camp and made new friends with kids from different towns and villages. We always exchanged letters throughout the school year: it was a great experience.

As a family we did not travel much. Mostly we would go on day trips. People in Slovakia rarely travelled and not many of them owned cars; we were no exception. We never owned a car, and so we traveled by train or bus.

Today I reflect back. I enjoyed that part of my life. Those days I was experiencing my True Self, exploring fully what life had to offer, playfulness and freedom.

Chapter Three

Late seventies...

My fifteenth birthday was fast approaching. Big changes, that I was not yet aware of, were heading my way.

It was my last year of elementary school. I needed to decide what I wanted to do in life. It was time to choose a school. I knew I liked to create, to do something with my hands and to work with people. I had a vision of a life of freedom and adventure. I saw everything as good and easy. A few people I knew told me to take off my rose-colored glasses, but that never resonated with me. I did not believe life was supposed to be a struggle in any way. In my family, and the families of my friends, there were issues and misunderstandings; however, I always felt love and strong connections underneath. I preferred to see what was good in people and I always felt there was much more to life than people realized.

Now I know the feelings I experienced then were happiness, deep wisdom, adventure and the celebration of life: full expression of my Soul.

When it was time to apply for college, my teachers asked me which school I wanted to attend. In my mind I heard hairdresser. I always liked combing and styling my grandmother's hair, while she told me stories about her life—moving, interesting stories. I loved my grandmother's stories of how the elders in their village helped the sick through natural remedies—how children were born at home and not in the hospital. I liked to listen to these stories while my hands were lost in her long hair. My grandma was a wise woman and she worked hard in her life. She had four children, my mother and three sons; the eldest lived in Canada and she often talked about him; the second son lived in our town, my mother was the third child, and the youngest son died as a young child.

When I was younger I had wanted to be a nurse so I could take care of people, but this changed when I witnessed my grandmother's suffering before she died. I was fourteen and I felt so much of her pain that it changed my mind. Then I dreamed of becoming a flight attendant, so I could travel and see the world.

One summer night, I was lying on the grass watching the stars and dreaming about my life. I wished to experience the world. Unfortunately, the communist regime in my country limited people, especially those like my family. Nobody from my family was a party member, so there was little possibility of traveling to another country, going to better schools, or learning other languages. Sometimes I questioned my dreams. What could I do or be? I was a small-town girl with big dreams; dreams I was unsure how to fulfill. Still, I kept dreaming and imagining trips to new places in my mind. Only I knew what was in my heart and in my dreams. These dreams felt real.

Many times I preferred to be in my dream world rather than the physical world. My dream world was peaceful, loving, and unlimited compared to the reality where people had problems, felt stuck and unhappy. Their limited beliefs of the world never resonated with me. My faith in something greater was strong; I continued to question life and to believe in everyone's goodwill.

My parents did not like the idea of me becoming a hairdresser. I know they wanted the best for me. They said they preferred that I work in an office where I would not have to stand all day. I kept quiet, but I was thinking, Oh no! Office work was the last thing I wanted to choose. Just thinking about it bored me. I did not see myself sitting in an office; I saw myself creating something with my hands and interacting with people. At the same time, I thought I should trust my parents, so I applied to the school they wanted, for the sitting job that just did not feel like me. In the end, the course had over three hundred applicants and only sixty openings. My father was not a communist, he did not belong to the party, so I knew deep inside I would not be a successful applicant. And that was perfectly fine with me. I did not want to go there. The question was, where do I go?

What I learned I was not accepted into the clerical program, I was relieved, but there were few options and not much time left. My father asked an acquaintance, who worked as a horticultural teacher, if he could help me to get in to the school where he taught: I soon learned this was the school I would attend. The word horticultural did not sound interesting to my ears, but I was young with not much life experience. I felt I had no other options my parents would approve. I was uninformed and naïve. It seemed that my dreams had come to an end and that I needed to face reality. I started trusting others more than myself. I believed my parents knew better than me, so I listened to them and I pushed away my true feelings. In an attempt to find something good about the situation, I made up a little story for myself, about working in a beautiful flower shop where I would create wedding bouquets because that was what I wanted to equate with horticulture. I liked the idea of working with my hands and fragrant flowers – gifts of nature – and seeing people happy when they received beautiful flowers. In my mind I created a reason to go to that school.

The challenge was that I would have to live there all week because it was too far to travel every day. I liked being home with my family even though I saw myself as an adventurist and a traveler. Most of all, I liked the freedom my parents allowed me to have. I wasn't comfortable with structure, and this course would mean the same structure every day. While I liked new things, I preferred to be in charge of my time. I wanted to explore and to not follow someone's commands. Although I liked being prepared and organized for school the best I could, and I liked keeping my room tidy and having clean clothes, I did not want anyone else to tell me when and how to do this. I knew how to manage on my own; that was my attitude from a very young age.

My parents were great people. They were loving and caring, and they allowed us freedom. They always wanted the best for us and they did the best they could. Sometimes my parents' focus on work, and on the challenges they faced while building the new house, taking care of three kids and my grandparents, their vineyard and their garden, made them forget to see their own greatness. Their parents had lived much the same way. Generation after generation believed in working so hard that they were too busy to see their greatness and uniqueness. Many times they saw each other's personalities instead of their loving hearts.

Looking back, most of the time people's focus was on work, and surviving the difficulties of life the human mind can create. I know my parents were seeking a different life, but they never took action to change it. Instead, they just kept busy, perhaps it was easier. Today, I am grateful for this understanding. It may not be easy to go within. It may be painful. Now I understand why, at times, it may be easier to keep busy in life. I believe that to feel our greatness, uniqueness, and the gifts of our souls we also must feel the pain we experienced in the past and past lives and release it—and that takes courage.

My fifteenth birthday arrived on a warm, lovely June day. I felt mature, not that I really knew how mature people felt. In my new maturity, I knew I wanted to face the world, my new life in a new school with everything it had to offer. I went to school that morning with a renewed sense that my life was unfolding before me. With only two weeks left in my present school, where I had spent more than half of my life attending, I was excited for the new experience at a new school. I did not think about the unknown and any challenges it would offer—it was all part of the adventure. The biggest change, I knew, would be spending each night away from my home, but I was ready to face any challenge as it arose. I was living my truth in my childish way. That day, my older brother's classmate came over; he had brought me a puppy. We never talked about dogs and I never wanted one, yet there he was. My parents were surprised, and so was I. I was hoping my parents would let me keep him. With boarding school in the fall, I was not sure the dog could be mine. We thought about finding him another home but after a couple of days he had already become a part of the family. I named him Rexo.

I never forgot that birthday. Looking back, I feel Rexo came to my family as a replacement for my presence in our home. I always looked forward to Fridays when I could see my family and Rexo. I did not spend much time with him, but he was my dog.

Chapter Four

Big change in my life...

Summer's end arrived; time to pack. It was time to start on my new educational path—horticultural school. I did not know what to expect, but I knew things would work out. Excited about meeting new people, I enjoyed the bus trip to my new school. My parents traveled with me on this first trip, leaving me with mixed feelings when they left for home.

At the beginning, it was strange for me to be there—alone. I felt like I was living in a box. There were four girls, strangers, in a room half the size of the bedroom I shared with my sister at home. Everything happened at the same time every day, breakfast, lunch, study time, dinnertime, bedtime. I always seemed to be standing in line in the dining room. It took some time for me to get used to the new routine. I often wondered how I would handle it for the next few years; definitely not what I would have preferred, but I was there.

Soon I realized I liked the school hours and enjoyed most of the subjects. We learned about plants, trees, flowers, and how to arrange them. We spent much of our time outdoors. A greenhouse on the school property contained many different plants, and there was a large park populated with evergreens, various bushes, and trees with apples we could pick for our lunch. It was the students' responsibility to care for the park grounds. One day a week we would do some planting and gardening. Life was exciting and good.

The classroom building had once been a monastery; it was old and lovely, and class-time compensated for the time afterward when things became boring for me. After some time, I found a balance and I felt I could handle this new lifestyle. The students were mostly girls and I made many friends in a short time. Before I knew it, the second year had passed. In my third year, my best friend, Viera, and I were old enough to commute to and from school each day. So we both moved back to our family homes and travelled to school together. I was up at five every morning and traveled by bus for an hour-and-a-half one-way. It was not always easy, but it worked for me. At the end of my three-year program, I realized I had truly enjoyed this time in my life. I made many friends and I learned a lot through new experiences. I learned to drive a tractor and a car and I got my driver's license at the end of the school year. I learned many practical things and I realized I liked to work in the garden and be in nature. I felt a connection to the plants, so I decided to attend school for two more years.

My last two years of school were in a different city, too far for a daily commute, but I was old enough to live on my own and make my own decisions. I thought I needed more education in my field to have a better job in the future. I started my new program as my life continued to unfold. I was eighteen, working part-time in a local greenhouse, happy with my life, and seeing a bright future on the horizon. I never stopped dreaming about traveling and exploring the world. My dreaming world was as real as reality.

Thoughts were jumping through my mind about life in Canada; this was my big dream, the one I did not think would ever come true.

All through school I dreamed about traveling. I loved adventure and exploring new places, and I was always excited about school trips. I liked listening to the few people, lucky enough to have traveled, talk about their trips to Western Europe, and about life there—it seemed as though people lived more freely in countries without borders. My mom's brother lived in Canada and regularly sent us pictures: I wondered about life there.

Besides the desire to travel, I had an urge, a feeling deep within that I wanted to move to Canada. I told my friends in school that I would one day go to Canada, though it seemed like a joke even to my ears. It was not easy to obtain papers for travel to western countries. I even questioned myself—what would I do there? I did not speak any language but my mother's, but I continued dreaming and talking about this dream. Luckily, my friends did not take me seriously—a good thing in a communist country. It was dangerous to talk about leaving. For years, I kept dreamed of leaving Slovakia and living in Canada: this dream always felt right to me.

Chapter Five

Falling in love...

I fell in love with a young man who I met while I was working at my part time job. One year after we met, I was pregnant and finishing my two-year school program. We were young, with not much life experience, but we were responsible for our situation and for the baby on the way.

Today I understand that everything in life happens for a reason and our daughter Daniela was a gift of God.

We married and lived with my husband's mother and sister. His father had passed away before we met. We both had jobs, but there were no apartments available. It was not unusual for people to wait for years before finding an apartment. I wanted us to have our own nest, but in the meantime we managed the best we could.

I liked my new family life as it was and happily waited for our baby's birth. I did not miss my single life. I envisioned and hoped everything would work out for us even though we had not planned on marriage and a family so soon. Our precious daughter, Daniela, was born at the end of February. Holding her in my arms for the first time was a moment I will never forget—it felt like I held the whole world in my arms: this reminded me of what my mother had said about how she felt when I was born. Daniela was a healthy, happy and beautiful baby. Our daughter was the first grandchild on both sides. She was loved and very special to our family; a sweet, precious miracle. She brought joy to everyone's heart.

Looking back thirty years, I now understand everything was part of the Divine's plan. Our daughter's Soul wanted us to be her parents. If not, it would be otherwise. I am blessed and fortunate to be a mother to the amazing woman my daughter is. I am thankful beyond words.

We were young, in our early twenties; my husband was only a few years older than I was. He wanted to spend time with his friends after work and not so much with us. I did not understand this. Many times I felt as though we did not share the same vision for our life, but we did not know how to communicate our challenges. Even though I felt life had more to offer than I was experiencing, I pushed these feelings aside. We tried our best, and were fortunate because both of us had good jobs and could support ourselves. After a year of living with my husband's mother, we were lucky to get a newly built apartment not far from her home. Although I liked my mother-in-law, I was happy to have our own place. She was a good woman and had suffered through many challenges in her life. I admired her strength, her devotion and her service to her family.

We moved into our apartment. After work, I kept busy caring for my daughter and decorating our new home. After work, my husband would often go out with his friends. While I waited for him with Daniela, I told myself he was young and wanted to be with his friends, but we were a family and I wanted us to spend time together. As time went by, I felt alone. My feelings were telling me something I was afraid to acknowledge. I handled this situation the best I could, but heaviness settled on my shoulders. I tried to make it easier. I tried to understand our situation and our feelings for each other. I looked for answers, for a solution. I wanted us to be a happy family. I wanted our marriage to work. I wondered why this was happening. We had a beautiful daughter and I wanted her to be happy with both of us. I wanted her to grow up with a mom and dad, as I had.

Late at night I would sit in our living room on my own, while Daniela slept in her bedroom. I would wait for my husband to come home…and wait some more. It did not feel right for me to be alone. Even though I was married, I felt like a single mother. I wished the three of us would spend time together, playing, having fun after we got home from work. It did not happen often. As I sat knitting, thoughts flowing through my mind, I questioned: What am I going to do? What can I do to make this work? I acknowledged we were young, maybe too young, but I loved home, family life, being a mother and wife and taking care of my family. It did not feel right being married and being alone. As I asked myself, my questions were answered, I heard: go, leave, leave. But I did not know where to go. It didn't feel right to move back in with my parents. They offered me the option when they saw I was unhappy but I wanted to be responsible. I wanted to have my own place and family. I wanted to live my life the way I envisioned. I had dreams and visions of marriage and family even though I had not planned it so early in my life. I wanted our marriage to work.

I tried talking to my husband about my feelings, but there was no clear communication between us. We were young, perhaps naïve about family life. Spending most evenings alone I began listening to music, the same music over and over again. It was an English album and I did not understand what they sang, but it eased my feelings. The music made me feel happy and stronger, more able to cope with being alone with my thoughts and questions. The repeated question 'What am I going to do?' echoed in my mind, and I continued to hear: go. One day the voice was clear: leave, emigrate. Oh God, I always dreamed about it, but obviously I had never left my country when I was single and my life was easy. How could I now do that with a small child? I wanted to make my relationship work and I wanted Daniela to have a father, but the more I fought my feelings the stronger they returned. I continued to question myself, and— again and again—I heard: go, go, emigrate with your daughter.

Many questions raced through my mind. Was my unhappy marriage a reason to go and live my dream? Was leaving the way for my dream to come true? Was it possible? It was almost too much to think about it. Why was I thinking of emigrating with my daughter? I was twenty-three and she was three. Could I do it? How would I do it? All these thoughts struck my mind over and over again…for months. To leave—to emigrate seemed like the only right answer. I just had no idea how I could make it possible, but it felt right in my core. All I could do was to trust.

Chapter Six

Decision made...

I stopped pushing my husband to do something he, perhaps, was not ready for, or not meant to do. I cannot change others; I can only change my life. I started dreaming again, like my teenage self.

Through my life challenges, I did the best I could. After less than a year of maternity leave, it was time to return to work. I had signed a three-year contract with the company I worked for because they paid my school tuition. I liked my job working with flowers in the greenhouse, but hoped for a better position one day. Before my contract ended, I experienced health issues. Often sick, the doctor advised me to stop working in the greenhouse. The company offered me a position in the office, replacing a woman who immigrated to Germany. What a coincidence. Although I preferred working with people and nature and knew the office job would not excite me, I took it, open to exploring new things. I quickly learned the job and enjoyed it while it was fresh and new. After a year I lost interest—same desk, same chair, same papers, and same three women doing the same thing all day long. I longed to create. I needed to do something with my hands, interact with people, move my body, see different scenery, see flowers blooming and smell their fragrance. That was me. Again I felt as though I was in a box, like when I started boarding school. I struggled with getting myself to work every morning. Not happy at work, or home, I continually told myself I would make it work—I would make it all work. All the while, I pretended everything was okay. I went to work, cared for Daniela, did the housework, and cooked meals for my family. During my alone time,

I played my favorite music and I dreamed my secret dream. I saw myself living in Canada. The memories of dreaming dreams, of escaping when I was in school, returned. Big dreams: watching the stars at night, seeing the vastness of the space above, feeling the fresh air as it entered my body when I breathed—so vast and open, so free, so beautiful.

Life was beautiful no matter what was going on, I knew this truth... and I could always dream. Nobody could stop me from dreaming.

My health and inner-strength returned. I created a plan in my dreams. Slowly, I sensed purpose in my life again. I felt I was on the right path. Although it was only in my imagination, it felt real to me—many times better than my physical reality. I created whatever I wanted in my imaginary life. I started believing in my dreams again and, for the first time, it did not feel like a joke; it had gradually felt less like a dream and more like reality. I had a plan and I would follow it. I had a call. It was not only for me but for my daughter, too. In my dream we were going... we were leaving...I had a clear vision of my freedom.

During this time, one of the two men, who worked in the office next to mine, returned from a trip to Canada where he was visiting his son. I listened closely as he shared stories about his visit in Canada, wanting to know more. As he spoke, I felt as though I was already there. Excited by his words, they encouraged me to find a way to go to this country. Even though I had no concrete plan or any knowledge of how to move to Canada, I knew I had to do this.

Now I understand all the synchronicities throughout my life. The Universe was preparing my path, my Divine mission to complete. All those experiences were written by my Soul before I was born. This is my understanding of my life.

The other man, in the next office, was a few years older than I was and, though I did not know why, I felt an urge to talk to him about the things that were happening in my life. I did not know him; I saw him only a few times before and we had never really talked, but there was something about him. I felt I could trust him. I sensed he would understand me. There was a connection between us that I could not understand. It was very strange, but I felt I could be my true self in his presence. I felt that he wanted to talk to me as much as I wanted to talk to him. I found out his name was Attila. The time came when I shared my feelings with Attila; all the while I wondered why I was doing this. When I spoke, he listened with interest. I told him about my secret plan to leave the country, my job and my marriage. It seemed unusual to open up to this man I barely knew; yet, at the same time, it felt natural, especially when he shared his own dreams and feelings. It felt like I found a long-time friend; this feeling was a true mystery to me...

Dealing with many life challenges, I welcomed the opportunity to share my innermost thoughts and feelings with a colleague, a friend who understood. It was liberating to discuss my plans. The feeling to leave the country with my daughter grew stronger with each passing day. I could not imagine how I would make this happen. I just knew that it would happen. It was time for us to go. And leave everything behind.

Chapter Seven

Opportunity of a lifetime...

Not a day passed when I did not dream of leaving the country. How this would happen, I had no idea. I wanted badly to go and, sometimes, I felt as though I was already there. Late one evening, I remember sitting home alone—again—on the balcony of our eleventh floor apartment. As Daniela slept, I watched the night city: buildings, streetlights, and cars on the roads. I imagined that the city below was a city in Canada. It felt right, exciting. I went to bed with the feeling of living in Canada in my heart. The next day at work I discovered our company was organizing a trip to Yugoslavia. They did it every few years. In fact, my husband and I had gone before.

I had heard that people could emigrate through Yugoslavia. Yes, the opportunity to leave had arrived. I would do everything to go... the time had come. I knew.

As I am sitting here at home in Canada writing this book, my feelings are taking me back to my early twenties, the time when I wanted to emigrate. At the time, emigration seemed to be the only way to deal with my situation. It was the spring of 1987. I knew it would be a great challenge, but I was ready to face it. Now I know every challenge we overcome, makes us stronger. It is the beauty of life to know this truth.

Chapter Eight

Trip with no return...

We were sitting on the bus to Yugoslavia. For my colleagues it was a vacation, but my plan was different. My plan was to stay, not to return home. My husband agreed to let Daniela come with me to Yugoslavia. It was a perfect chance to escape, a way to leave behind my dysfunctional marriage, the job I disliked, and a way to realize my strong calling. I always felt in my heart that my place in the world was elsewhere. I loved my family, my parents and siblings, dearly, but my heart's call to leave was strong, nothing could stop it. It was an unexplainable feeling.

July fast approached, and I was packed and ready to go. I exchanged extra money because I knew I could not stay in Yugoslavia as a refugee. I would have to go to a different country from there, Italy or Austria, somewhere where there were refugee camps. I had some information, and I trusted everything would be revealed to me as I went. My inner feeling of trust was stronger than ever. I planned to go to Italy. I heard there were people in Yugoslavia that would sail those who wanted to immigrate to Italy for money. Some people were escaping through the tunnels in the mountains, while the trains were running. That sounded too risky for me; I could not place my daughter and myself in danger. I knew I had to leave and I knew I had to be careful and responsible for the choice I made for both of us. It would change our life forever.

It was time to say goodbye to my family. I do not know where I got the strength to do it. I do not know how I did it, but I did. I visited my parents and my siblings for the last time: my home town where I grew up. My family knew about my intention of leaving, it had been my dream since I was a teenager, but no one talked about it that day. Perhaps they did not believe I would escape, because I was only twenty-four years old with a four-year-old daughter. I knew I had to leave. I was leaving everything behind. The feelings of love for my family, and the memories of my childhood were so strong I had to block them that day, otherwise I would have been unable to leave…It was not easy. It was not easy at all.

The day had come. A day after I visited and said good-bye to my dear family I left my apartment with a suitcase in one hand and my daughter holding the other—and the plan to never return. We were ready to go on the bus waiting to take us to Yugoslavia. I had one more goodbye—my friend, Attila, from work—the only person who knew my plan. I do not know why I cared about this man. We shared some connection I did not understand. I felt he understood my pain, the reason I needed to emigrate. Perhaps it was because he held pain in his heart too. Perhaps he had big dreams like mine. Perhaps he understood my desire to be free and not live in a country with locked borders. He was there for me in the last few months. I felt he cared about me too…it was a strange feeling. I questioned why in my mind…but it was time to leave…without an answer. Saying goodbye to Attila would be one of the moments I would always remember.

I saw him briefly before the bus took off. I could feel our hearts' connect on a deep level. The feeling was so strong that it is hard to describe. I wondered how the feelings I shared with him could be stronger than the feelings I shared with my husband. If only I had the same connection with my husband, perhaps I would not have had a call to escape. Many mysterious and puzzling questions bombarded my mind: too many to deal with. I was twenty-four with big dreams, a young daughter and only a few hours left with this version of my life. I was leaving everything behind but my daughter. It would be only the two of us, sharing an unknown journey, and yet it felt real and right.

Soon I would be at the border and nothing from that life would be my reality anymore. I would be in a new country, breaking free of the past, with my greatest treasure—my child. I thought of all the dreams that mattered to me most at that moment of my life. I could no longer think about the life I was living or maybe I no longer wanted to. I held the image of my life of freedom strongly in my mind's eye. I would not give up.

I know now, Divine plan was in motion. The call of my heart was strong and it was a part of my Soul mission.

On the bus, I watched the buildings and trees as we drove by, everything looked the same as the times before, but nothing felt the same. It was as if time had stopped. I stared through the window. Strange. I had no comparisons for the feelings within. I never felt anything like this before. Feelings of release, comfort and expansion. Feelings of a mysterious journey.

In that moment, I owned nothing and had no address. I had only my daughter and myself. She sat next to me like a smaller version of myself—we even shared the same name, Daniela. Together, we would explore the unknown. I knew this was a big risk and an even bigger responsibility; not only for my life, but also for the life of my innocent little girl, who had no idea what was happening. With her happiness and playfulness and unconditional love, she was telling me she completely trusted and loved me. It was an amazing journey; just the beginning.

This was a big step in our lives, one I made for both of us. It felt right and amazing.

A new reality. Everyone on the bus looked happy. People were laughing, having fun, and looking forward to their vacation. My emotions were turbulent; I felt them in every cell of my body. I could not pretend to feel the excitement of a vacation. My mind spun with thoughts of escaping, revealing memories from my last visit with loved ones, knowing that I may not see them again. But I made the choice and was not returning home...it was my truth, I believed.

My mind and heart raced from emotion to emotion, not knowing which to settle on. I closed my eyes, held my daughter's hand, and tried to sleep. I wanted to forget about everything at least for a moment. I wanted rest so I could be strong, I would need it. Sleep failed me that early afternoon. The torturous feelings spinning through my body did not let me sleep. A sudden urge to go to the washroom grabbed me. It was not a physical need; I just needed to be alone for a moment. My body needed an emotional release, one I could not identify. Maybe laughing would help, maybe crying. I did not know and no one would understand, but I knew I wanted a little time to be on my own. I rose from my seat and walked up the bus aisle to the driver and asked if we could make a stop at a public washroom. He told me that we would stop in approximately fifteen minutes. I returned to my seat feeling some release from my emotions. Those few steps to the front of the bus and back gave me some comfort after all. I sat down next to my beautiful sleeping daughter, feeling a deep strength come over me, and instantly fell asleep

I awoke to silence. No one talked. Everything was still. For a moment, I forgot where I was. I felt relaxed. Looking through the window, I saw that we had arrived at the border. I saw a uniformed man and the police. Living in a communist country, borders were scary places to be. I watched through the window, curious and less emotional. The short sleep had helped me. The waiting seemed to take forever. I wanted to cross the border—cross into my new reality. Patiently, I waited with everyone else. Getting across was a formality as we were going on vacation. All of a sudden I heard my name called; the driver gestured me toward the front. What? I thought. No, no, I did not want to hear my name called at the border. Had someone reported my escape plans to the police? Were they taking me back home? Oh God no. It was not my home anymore; this much I knew without a doubt. What was happening? I believed that no one knew who would report me. Thoughts and feelings of fear stroked my body in a split second. I stood, my body felt heavy and stiff, not wanting to hear what they had to say. My inside voice said it is not true. Placing one foot in front of the other, I walked slowly toward the front of the bus. Seeing my life unfold in slow motion, I refused to believe this could be my truth. The driver stood at the front of the bus with a happy smile on his face. He said, "Here, you can go to the washroom." My spine was on fire, and sweat broke out all over my body. Oh, my God, thank you. I did not believe I could have survived being sent back. Sudden clarity washed over me. My home is somewhere else now. I did not know where, but I knew I was not returning.

I went to the washroom; I felt release as I took a deep breath. After I got back to the bus I felt better. I heard the motor running and I knew we had crossed the border. On my journey to my new life with my daughter, I felt the worst was over. I knew we would not stay in Yugoslavia, and I knew they could still make me return. However, things felt different. We had at least ten hours left of our drive. We would arrive by early morning. I could finally have the rest I needed. Holding my daughter's hand I wanted to sleep, I felt tired and strong at the same time...wondering where my home was.

Chapter Nine

My new life began with a sunrise...

I was ready, rested after a long night sleep on the bus. We had finally arrived at the hotel, a beautiful building with breathtaking views of the Adriatic Sea. I felt freshness in the warm morning air. The beach called us, and I wanted to go and play with my daughter. I needed to rest my mind. The next two weeks I would have to deal with a challenge that I had never dealt with before. I made a decision and the responsibility fully belonged to me. I had only two weeks to turn my plan into reality and I wanted at least two days to energize my body and rest my mind so I could be strong to walk my journey.

We played in the ocean, loving every minute. The water cleansed and soothed me. The day passed quickly, but we enjoyed every moment of it. We were happy to go to sleep. It felt good to be there with my daughter. I felt at peace as I looked forward to the next day. My mind slowed, my body relaxed. I knew I could do it. I knew it was meant to happen...my feelings were clear and loud. There was an unexplainable power in charge within me, and I trusted it. Before, my dreams felt like reality, now my reality felt like a dream. What is reality? I questioned.

Another new day—another beginning. I was more aware of this truth there than I was at home. Every morning was a new beginning, a new opportunity to love what I had and to approach everything unfolding in my life with faith. After breakfast, we returned to the beach again. It felt right to return. It felt like some strong energy moved my body—I did not resist, everything just felt right. I swam with Daniela again and, moment-by-moment my life was unfolding. That afternoon I began wondering whom I could possibly approach. Whom could I trust to tell my plan? I needed someone who could, and would, help me to get to a different country, where I could stay as a refugee. Then I could take the next step. I had an uncle in Canada; I would contact him and ask him for help with the next step. I knew he helped many emigrants there. Time was of the essence as I had only twelve more days. I had come this far. I was only steps away from what I had planned for years. This was it...my dream was becoming my reality. I was amazed and thankful.

The next morning I walked around the hotel property searching for someone to talk to. I was eager to meet someone who would give me more information. I did not speak their language, but could understand some because it was one of the Slavic languages, similar to my mother's. I hoped I would understand the language enough to get by. I had hope. I believed. I continued looking around, hoping to find someone who could help me, but I found no one. When I did come across people there was always someone from my office nearby. I could not do anything that would appear suspicious. I had to be careful, very careful. If one of my work associates reported me I could end up back home, possibly without a passport for the rest of my life. I could not risk that. I refused to think about it; instead I focused on my plan.

The next day, the hotel staff informed us of an organized trip to a neighboring town where we could visit the market and do some shopping. Yes, I believed this was my opportunity. There would be locals there, someone who could possibly help me. I visualized someone taking me and Daniela to Italy or Austria. I heard that is how people emigrated before. I had extra money, I could pay someone. I was prepared. It was a short trip, perhaps two hundred kilometers away...There had to be someone who would do it.

On the way to town, I was holding my plan in my heart, and my head was going in the speed of light. The only solid piece of the plan was the what. I didn't have the how worked out...I trusted that everything would fall into place. The plan I envisioned was stronger than fear, which was testing me and trying to win. The market place was a refreshing reality compared to the quiet seclusion of the hotel. My daughter enjoyed walking there, observing beautifully colored handmade crafts. Although she was not yet five years old, she admired art because she was artistic herself. Watching her joy I realized I felt love, freedom, and an appreciation for life. She pointed her little finger at a table with woven baskets. She asked for one. I let her choose her favorite, a small, dark brown basket. So involved seeing her happy, I had forgotten my plan for that moment... This small basket created much joy and fun, it was priceless.

Looking back now it was a lasting moment to always remember. It seems fresh even today, almost thirty years later. My daughter saved that little woven basket. She loved it so much; she still has it in her favorite toys collection.

As we walked around the market, enjoying the sights and sounds, my plan of emigration was strongly in my mind. Everywhere we went I expected to find the right person. The person I could trust who would help us to get out of Yugoslavia, to a different country, where the two of us could safely stay as refugees. Alert, fully focused, eyes wide, I felt the urge to approach the right person. Walking hand in hand with Daniela I could sense her discomfort. Did she know something was coming? I tightly held her hand, wondering how so many people could surround us yet I still felt as though no one could help. Despair filled my mind and I felt like I would collapse, but my inner-self stood strongly. I could not allow it to happen; I had to keep going. I chose to not give up. I chose my life, my hopes, and my dreams. I chose happiness for us. I chose to be free. My moment of despair passed as we continued walking. Continued hoping for a connection...for help. Continued looking for a face. Continued living my dreams. My truth was not giving up.

I wanted this done. I knew it was written in my life's script. I needed to go. This feeling was deeply rooted within me I could not help but feel it.

I could not ignore it. It existed as my body did: a strong feeling within. I could neither touch nor see it, but I sensed it so strongly it shook my core.

Every minute felt like an hour. The two of us walking together as one, walking tall, even though both of us were small, I felt our united strength. We were one powerful entity. My daughter was my strongest and only support on this journey. She was the one who helped me to take every step forward...her unconditional love, her innocence, the happy heart she offered every step we made together.

Oh, I love you, Dada, so much, words cannot describe. I am writing this book for you to know what we were going through and I feel the eternal love between us that I will cherish forever.

Changes had taken shape quickly. Time grew shorter for the opportunity to leave, but the closer I came to achieving my vision every moment seemed to slow. I saw a little girl running toward us fast, when just earlier everything felt as if it were slow motion. I recognized her from our bus. Her mother followed closely behind, she worked where I did, although I did not know her well. I hoped not to see any of my travel companions while we were out. I did not have time for this interaction. I wanted to meet someone I did not know, someone who could get Daniela and me safely out of this country, where we could find a refugee camp. And no one from our travel group could help... Oh God, why?

The girl wanted the basket from my daughter and pulled it from her hands. Daniela cried, when she never cried. Never. Her reaction surprised me. In this moment, her crying symbolized my uneasy feelings, feelings I was unable to express. I realized the sense was the same one I had experienced earlier; she knew something was coming. I knew I had to be there for her, more than in the physical sense. I wanted to be there for her emotionally; my mother's instinct guided me. My mind held me in despair, but I could not show it. I could not cry out loud, even when I wanted to, badly. Why was this happening now? Frozen inside, acting like nothing was happening; I pretended everything was okay...When I felt nothing was okay. My plan was not taking shape. My inner voice deep within me whispered I should return to my hotel room. I wanted to ignore it, yet, I returned to the hotel for my daughter. I was suffering enough in my life. I did not want her to suffer.

Back at the hotel room, my thoughts were mixed, senseless. Deep inside, I felt I had made the right decision to return. I needed a different plan, but nothing new surfaced. My mind blanked, offering no answers, no guidance. Instead, it replayed memories of the afternoon, followed by everything in my life prior to those moments. It showed my plan for the future, my plan to emigrate. The urge in my heart to leave this country gained strength. It had to happen... My mind reminded me of my plan, soothing my chaotic emotions; simply telling me there was nothing to be done at that moment, telling me to relax when I was tired of thinking. Daniela was already fast asleep. My thoughts slowed down, comforted by my heartbeat, and I told myself that for the moment everything was okay. I felt the comfort of this truth. Tomorrow would be a new morning, a new beginning, a new chance...time to follow my heart, my plan.

When I awoke, my feelings and my inner voice scared me. I suddenly had thoughts of returning home. No, oh no, I thought. I did not want to go back to Slovakia. It did not feel like home anymore...or did it? I had left everything behind. Although I loved my parents, my siblings, my family and the country I grew up in, I could not go back to that life. I had a call to change my life. I did not see myself going back to an unhappy marriage or back to a job I had not chosen for myself; it did not fulfill me. It was not easy to find a better job in the communist regime. I did not know any big people who could help me find a better job. I did not feel free there. I had a vision of creative work, travel, exploring life, but it was almost impossible to travel from my country. Most people spent their lifetime in the same town. Many times, I questioned myself why I had such visions, and why I wanted to live them? Is it possible? Others had dreams, and they did not live them, and many had no visions for their life. Why did I have such a strong urge to do something else in a country I had never seen before? Canada was so far away...Some of my friends told me to take off my rose-colored glasses. They said I could not wear them in real life. They told me to live in reality. But I saw my reality in a different way than they saw theirs. I was not afraid to live my life fully and to have my own dreams. Why was I different? Why did I have these visions and why did I want them to be my reality?

The thought of what to do consumed me. I could not give up. I did not want to. I wanted to live my dreams, not just dream them. I could do it—I repeated to myself. I would do it. I dreamed, I hoped and I trusted that I would find the way. I knew there must be a way. I had more time—it was good to know. There was hope. I trusted.

We returned to the beach, the unknown energy pushed me there again. I sat there staring at the water. Daniela was not comfortable; she cried again. We left the beach for the swimming pool so she could play with other children, but she cried even more. I could not understand why she cried, and she could not explain it to me. Her crying was strange to me. I did not know what to think about her crying, but I knew it was telling me something. I felt I had no choice, but to let go. Let go of my plan? I tried to push away thoughts about going back home. I stopped thinking about emigration. I stopped thinking about my plan. I was not even thinking about the vacation. I refused to think about the pain of the past and big dreams of the future. The present moment was all that existed. My truth was now. I knew. As I stared at the water, I heard my inner voice telling me, go home, go home, everything is okay...go home, everything is okay...you will see. I doubted this voice because it challenged all that had brought me to Yugoslavia, but I could not doubt the feeling of peace accompanying the thought. My thoughts were confused. On the one hand, they told me I had failed, and on the other, they told me it is okay to go back home. Although it was a painful experience listening to my thoughts, deep inside I knew returning home did not mean I had given up. I was guided to return; I do not know why... In my heart I knew that one day I would emigrate and live my dreams. It had to be my destiny; otherwise I would not have felt it so strongly. Perhaps the timing was not right... Perhaps it was not safe for us to go from here...I felt Daniela's cry was a sign. I did not know what it was, I just realized this was my new truth, and it was not easy to look at... it was disappointing. I chose to return, following the whispering voice, again. I will be going home, facing what I left forever, I thought.

As I look back now, I was not fully experiencing the feelings of disappointment because I pushed them away. I had to re-experience them and feel them fully, to be able to recognize them and put them into words and release them from my energy field. As I did, I completed my healing—emotional healing of that part of my life. At the time, I had to push away many of my feelings to be able to go through the experience.

The second week flew by. Moments of disappointment and desperation crowded my mind because I had to return home. But feelings of love, strength, hope, and belief in my dreams were stronger. Life was beautiful; I needed only to remember the precious time I spent with my daughter under the sun by the Adriatic Sea. These feelings helped me stumble through the rest of my so-called vacation. Packing our suitcase, for our return to the home I thought I had left forever, gave me a bittersweet memory of our vacation. The home that was familiar to me, the only one I had ever known, was strange and difficult to dwell upon, and especially difficult to return to. Two voices warred within me, creating a challenging existence. But I possessed hope and faith: the voice of my Soul. I had my daughter, and my life ahead of me. I was healthy, and believed in myself. I was not afraid of life's challenges. I knew I could live my dreams. I knew my dreams were for me to live, not only to dream. I trusted.

On the bus ride home, a feeling of bliss emerged in my body, making me realize I was happy to be coming home. I pictured the reunion with my parents and my siblings and my daughter's happiness when she saw her grandparents. Strong feelings arose within me when I thought of my friend, Attila, and our deep connection. I questioned reality, again and again. Why did I have these unexplainable feelings for him? I knew he had a family, but I could not help but feel I had known him before, perhaps in another life? It felt so strange. It would be a challenge to face it all again. How could I live my life from now on? It was difficult to imagine. My mind was blank. All I knew was that my life was a big mystery, a big puzzle, with me in the middle.

It was a beautiful, sunny summer day when we crossed the border back into Slovakia. The warm feelings during the trip home had been eclipsed by a deep silence within, I knew I would try again...I would escape. At that moment, I buried all my feelings because there were just too many to deal with. I was grateful for Daniela; she was the spark in my life. Her soft voice, her laughter and happiness kept me going. I was busy with her life. I felt a responsibility to keep her safe and happy. At the same time, my urge to emigrate continued—after we had returned it grew even stronger. The moment I stepped off the bus I knew, I had only come back to put my papers together. This time we would go straight to Austria where we could claim refugee status. I KNEW I would do everything in my power to leave as soon as possible. The worst scenario meant one more year...it seemed like forever. I needed to be strong to do this. I kept repeating the words, I AM. I would be; I had promised myself.

Chapter Ten

Am I home...

Once home, I felt like a stranger everywhere I went. When it was time to return to work, everyone asked about my trip. If they only knew the truth of my situation...I had an opportunity to escape, but I had failed. Did I? I had no words to describe the vacation. I foresaw at least another year before I could attempt leaving again...again...again was my truth.

When I saw my friend from the office, my heart started beating like a drum. My feelings were strong, almost overwhelming. I had never felt anything like this before. What were these feelings? Why did I feel this way? I completely trusted him. He knew my plan and I trusted he would not say a thing to anyone. I wanted desperately to tell him my experience and share my feelings with him, but I could not. There were people everywhere, who would see everything. This friendship, I sensed, would not make it easy for me to leave. I pushed my feelings aside and covered them up. I had to focus on my plan, it was important to me.

I had no idea how to put my papers together. Communism complicated the exercise. Knowing powerful people in the regime or community helped, unfortunately, I knew no one in these positions. I felt like a complete outsider. But I knew I would never give up my dream. Days passed, and I was no further ahead because I did not know where to begin. I dreamed my dreams for weeks after our return from Yugoslavia and continued struggling to find a starting point. Then one early autumn day, a group of people celebrating a birthday in my office were discussing travel, and my starting point was revealed. I believed I had found someone who could help. The gentleman in our department knew someone in the application office, someone who could help me and my daughter get into Austria. Wow. This was an exciting surprise. Not many people had connections in these places. My new concern was whether my application would appear suspicious and whether this person would tell anyone else at work. I did not jump on the opportunity right away. Instead, I listened, observed, and decided to give this new information some time to sink in. I would ask him later, if I felt I could trust him. By the time I arrived home from work that day, the situation dominated my thoughts and I decided not to wait and planned to ask him the next day. He was willing to help me. I was amazed. It felt as though I had found the way; the right way. I trusted that my daughter and I would emigrate for sure this time. It had to be.

I had to be careful in how I approached the application. I could not create suspicion. I told him I wanted to visit Austria because I loved exploring new places and, since it was less than an hour and half bus ride, I thought it was a perfect place for a vacation. The travel application and passport were not easy to obtain, but I refused to see this as an obstacle. I chose to view my situation as an adventure. I had to try everything within my power to enable my dreams—I had faith. But I had to wait until January to apply, and then at least another four months to find out if the government would let us go.

During the waiting period, I would have to prepare additional paperwork that was needed for me to travel, specifically, permission from Daniela's father to allow her to travel with me. It was another challenge I could not immediately see my way through. I decided that I would face it later. I had been handed a second chance and, this time, I would not return home. Deep within I felt it.

I felt it would be a challenge to ask my husband, as I had once told him I would leave him, and emigrate from our homeland. He had not believed me then and I wondered whether he thought I would do it now. Time was ticking away, I finally asked him because I had no choice. To my surprise, he displayed no concerns toward my request and signed the paperwork.

Looking back now, I could see how the emigration was a part of my life journey. It was part of a Divine plan how everything worked in my favor, even when I felt it extremely challenging at that time.

As my twenty-fifth birthday approached, I was ready to go. Far more ready than the year before. When I travelled to Yugoslavia, the year before, I had taken only the hope to emigrate with me. This time I would travel with certainty, and a deep knowing that my daughter and I were leaving forever. By the end of June, the application had been approved. I had exchanged money and had my papers together. I was ready to go, again. This time it was different, because this time it was not only my daughter and me. Attila had decided to join us. I discovered, as we grew closer, he had his own long time calling to emigrate. He shared with me that when he was young he always wondered where he would be in twenty or thirty years, because he knew he would not be home. He knew he would be in a different country. Just like me. He lived through his own challenges getting his paperwork together. I would never have thought this could happen when I met him.

Everything that was happening in my life seemed unbelievable, and it was all happening so fast. It was the end of August. Within the next few weeks, after some formalities, we would leave. That was our plan. When I started packing, I knew that my future would be much different than the one I had planned two years ago when I had first decided to emigrate. I trusted life as it unfolded, because it felt right.

Chapter Eleven

The day I will never forget...

On September 26, 1988, the sun shone on our new beginning. I took my daughter to preschool in the morning, and then went to work as though nothing out of the ordinary was planned. I was careful not to appear suspicious before leaving the soil of our home country. We still had a few hours before we could leave. I had to finish some work in the office and it was hard for me to concentrate enough to get it done. At lunchtime I left my workplace, pretending my daughter had a doctor's appointment. It was my last day at work. I felt expansion knowing that. I picked up my daughter and went to our apartment for the last time.

Attila came over and we put two suitcases in the car, some food and drinks and, with less than one thousand dollars in our pockets, we drove to the border. My daughter slept peacefully on the back seat as we drove away from our past. We were ready to cross the border. This new truth of mine felt like a dream, like a movie. It seemed only yesterday I had crossed the border into Yugoslavia, but it had been more than a year. The feelings coursing through my body were different this time. We were going, we were ready and we were driving to Austria. This time, when we approached the border, I felt certain my plan would be completed. Austria was a safe place to stay.

Had I been pushed to return home last year, by unseen forces, so we could go together now? I questioned.

It was 2:15 pm, a warm sunny afternoon when we reached the border. A moment forever kept in our memory, deeply in our Souls. The border authority asked us questions, checked our luggage, and the car. We remained calm, careful; anything else could jeopardize our crossing. This magical moment had arrived, and with it came much tension. The door to Austria was a hundred meters ahead. We saw our freedom in the distance, the beginning of our new path together within view.

Twenty minutes later—not much time in the span of our lives—the authority guard let us cross. I had dreamed of seeing the world since I was a teenager and it was finally coming true. At that moment I felt every fiber of my body, as I had never felt before. It was indescribable. Images and feelings flooded my consciousness. All my dreams would soon be replaced with reality, because we were in Austria. We were in Austria. In Austria. My eyes were wide open. And I repeated that sentence in my head...In Austria. We were speechless as we drove through the countryside. Was it real? Were we really together? It felt so different than seeing each other at work. It felt as if we had lived together before and we were going home. Hmm...Suddenly, a question whispered through my mind...Will Attila stay? Attila's paperwork allowed him five days of vacation, while mine allowed twenty. What if he decided to go back home? I felt he would stay. Either way, I knew I would stay. My home was here.

While driving to Vienna, we planned to call my uncle in Canada to get information. I could not call him while I was home, nor could I ask through the mail. It was too great a risk as the communists were monitoring calls and mail. Vienna, the capital of Austria, was a beautiful city and not too far. We parked the car, and then bought a map of Austria so we could figure out how to get to the refugee camp, and then we made the phone call. We had to get to the camp as soon as possible to find a place to sleep, because we did not want to spend money to stay at the hotel. We did not know what was ahead of us, so we wanted to keep the money we had. It was at least a three-hour drive to the camp and the evening sky was getting dark. We decided to make the drive the next morning. We found a small park and ate some food we had brought from home. Daniela did not ask any questions, almost as though she understood what was happening. There were no tears this time. I was surprised at how she handled this escape and I was totally amazed by how happy she was.

We stayed in Vienna and slept in the car at a parking lot close to the airport. Our first night in our new, temporary home, we were lucky to have a car to sleep in. The fact that we were in Austria and we were beginning our journey was everything we could ask for at that time. In the morning, we would take another step, totally unknown. I trusted.

Chapter Twelve

First day of our life in Austria...

We awoke to a lovely, sunny morning. It mattered little that the car seats were not comfortable for sleeping. We were excited to start our new journey despite the unknown. After freshening up in a nearby public washroom, we ate a small breakfast in the car, and were soon off toward the camp.

Driving through the countryside, along curving roads, we were amazed by the beauty of nature, the mountains, and rivers. We had no idea what lay ahead of us that day, the next, a week later, or even a year. All we knew was what we had right then, in the moment, what we felt, and what we wanted from the future. That moment was magical, and we held on to it as though it was all that mattered. It was.

We came upon the town of Traiskirchen, turning up and down different streets, hoping to find the refugee camp. We did not know in which part of town the camp was situated, but Attila trusted his intuition, and drove us right to it. We needed to register with the camp to remain in Austria. It was the first, and most important, step we needed to make. When we arrived we were shocked. A huge, old military building housed the camp, and outside at least two hundred people lined the fence in front of the building. Some looked like they had been waiting a long time. They built shelters along the sidewalk from paper boxes and waited with their belongings with despair on their faces. We saw many families with small children. Stunned by the scene, I said nothing. Attila and I looked at each other in shock, observing, but not speaking. I, we, had not expected to see this scene...At all.

Parking nearby, we walked toward the long line up to see what was going on. We did not speak the German language, and had only a pocket dictionary I had brought from home. I knew we would need it. I held Daniela's little hand tightly in the crowd. She remained cooperative and said nothing, which made it easier for me. With her limited understanding of our situation, I felt she had many questions. She was a curious child. I sensed her maturity and sometimes I thought of her as an adult in a child's body, and that was why she was the way she was when we arrived in Austria. I felt, deep inside, she knew...

We watched as police officers at the front took peoples' passports and slowly let them in behind the fence, into the small office at the ramp. It took a long time with such a big line up. It seemed the line hardly moved since our arrival, but we had no other choice than to wait patiently. There was still the option to go back home without being charged for illegally leaving our country. Our papers were valid for vacation in Austria—but returning was not an option for us, not even in the silence of our thoughts. The decision we made was as real as our breath.

They took in a few more people before closing the gate. Promptly, at four o'clock the office closed. They would open the following morning. We stayed there for a little while and watched as people left, and others stayed close to their paper boxes on the sidewalk. What could we do? What should we do? We could not plan anything, not even one day ahead. We had to be patient and take every moment as it unfolded. It was not easy, but we did it. We wanted to. We returned to the car...thanking God we had one. Again, we ate in the car, and then we found a parking lot and waited for the sun rise. We could do nothing else.

I watched the sun rise through the trees from the car, ready to face another day at the refugee campsite. We had the whole day ahead of us and hoped to get in. Having no idea how the process worked, we could not help but wonder what went on behind the fence. The only thing we were sure of was how badly we wanted to get in. There was safety behind the fence. People there were accepted as refugees and they could start the process of applying to the country where they wanted to live. We had to get in. We hoped to get in. We wanted to get in. But how do we get in? These were the only thoughts on my mind although deep inside my heart I possessed no doubt we would get in.

Again, we patiently waited in line with many people from different countries, speaking their own languages. All of us with one hope – to get in. Behind the fence awaited a new life, a new beginning. Daniela, my daughter, coped amazingly well under the circumstances. In her child's mind she really had no idea what was happening. On that day, I carried paper and crayons for her. She spent the day drawing pictures, lost in her creative world. She was an incredible child.

Early afternoon came and went, and we were still quite a distance from the entrance. We met a family from our country. It was a comfort to hear someone speak our language. They had two small boys. Our children played together. Everyone needed help. So we shared information with those who could understand us. It felt like one big refugee family. One man asked whether we were from Czechoslovakia. I asked him how he could tell. He said he had noticed my shoes. People were searching for signs, anything that could help them connect with another. They wanted to talk, they wanted information, and they wanted to at least hear their own language.

Less than an hour before the gates were closed, our hope shrank. We were just too far down the line. It was a tough truth to know we would not get in that day. The line-up was too long; time was ticking. We were patient. It was the only way to make our situation easier. Four o'clock struck. The day was over for the office workers. It was time to head home to their families. That was life. Every choice had consequences. We made the choice to leave our homes. For the moment, our home was the car and we were fortunate and thankful to have it. Unlike many other families in line, we did not have to sleep outside on the sidewalk covered with boxes. It was the end of September; the days were warm and sunny and the nights were cooler. We enjoyed spending the day outside. Our hope to get into the camp did not come to fruition, but we had a good day. I admired the pictures Daniela drew. I hugged her, kissed her, and silently thanked her for being cooperative. I was thankful to God to have her and Attila in my life that moment. Gently holding her hand, we walked back to the car. Tomorrow, tomorrow will come fast.

Leaves were starting to fall from the trees. The outdoors felt good; the harvest was in the air. It felt like our day of hope had been delayed. Tomorrow—I told myself, tomorrow would be our day of hope. I realized that sometimes things in life come in different ways and at different times than expected. Hope never died. As we walked to our car, our temporary home, I sensed deep down that the following day would be the day; we would walk through the gates. The feeling of fearlessness, the deep knowing of my Soul amazed me, and it helped me hold up my head with confidence.

I feared nothing. It was a new day and a new beginning. After a long, cool night I was happy to see the sun shining. Daniela slept in the back seat, while Attila and I slept in the front seats. It was a long night. I did not sleep well. Over and over I awoke to stare at the dark night just beyond the windshield. Chilled and uncomfortable in my sitting position, I could do nothing but hope. I looked forward to lining up in the morning. In my mind I saw us getting through the gates. With this thought, I fell asleep again.

Looking back on that time now, I still recall the feeling of fearlessness and trust. The experience shaped me into the person I am today. I felt the depth of my freedom and the power of my naked essence of my Soul. It moved my body. In that time of owning almost nothing physical, I owned my own truth, my dreams, my strength, the love and gratitude in my heart for every given moment of the unknown and the vision for a new life. I totally trusted The Unknown as it unfolded, knowing all was well. It was.

Our third day of waiting in the line started like the others, only now time was of the essence as Attila's legal papers allowed for only two more days in Austria. Mine allowed for another seventeen days, but we knew we were in this together. We just had to get in. Even under this pressure we were calm and confident. Familiarity with the scenario helped, as did the beautiful weather and Daniela's abundant happiness. It felt as though the three of us created a strong bond in a very short time. The sense of supporting each other without words, just our presence, was immense. I felt this little girl of mine had a big role in this emigration process. I touched her dark silky hair, and looked into her big green eyes, savoring the moment. Knowing it would always stay in my memory, and so would her loving, smiling face, and her innocent childish beauty.

Time was going fast, already after noon, but the lineup had barely moved forward. Like yesterday, and the day before. I thought if the line moves as slowly as it had for the last two days it would take us two weeks to get into the camp. At two o'clock, my hope of getting in was fading but I refused to let go. I kept hope alive. Miracles happened and I believed in them. I had faith. We stood in the line, waiting, and not giving up. We had two more hours for a miracle to happen. Hope was present within me while tension silently moved throughout my body. Both feelings were deeply rooted. Waiting was the only option for us. There was nothing else we could do.

All of a sudden a police officer came out of the office to talk to the people in the crowd. Unfortunately, we could not understand what he said. We tried to understand, desperately wanting to know what he was saying. We hoped he would speak to us…maybe he would say something that could help us get in. One word caught our attention, the only one we understood—FAMILY. And then someone from the crowd spoke in a language we understood. The officer was calling families into the office. Oh my God! I knew we were going in. We pushed through the crowd, pushing Daniela ahead of us. We could not miss this opportunity. Attila took our passports and rushed to the front. We followed closely behind. There were other families pushing and pulling their children through the crowd. Tension filled the air, everybody wanted into the camp. We crossed through the gate with no time to think. Time had come to get ourselves into the office, it was almost four o'clock. Yes, finally, they were going to let us in. The officer took our passports and noticed our different last names. When he realized we were not a family, he questioned us. We were honest and told him we were not married, but we were together and wanted to stay together. He stared at us, but said nothing. Perhaps it was too late for him to deal with such a situation at the end of the day. Perhaps he felt compassion for us. Perhaps we looked like a family. We will never know what moved him to let us enter the camp that day, but he let us proceed. Relief swept through us. We were in. The miracle we were waiting for had happened. It was September 29, the day the door opened to our new life.

Looking back, I now know God was working behind the scenes for us, like he always does. Where there is the hope and belief in a miracle, it must happen. It cannot be otherwise. That moment was magical and promising. The officer handed us papers to sign; we had no idea what we were signing. We were escorted into the main building, and at that moment feelings of happiness and rebirth nearly overwhelmed us. We did not, for a moment, think we had stepped into the biggest, challenging test of our lives.

They kept our passports and took us to another office for a short interview with a translator. They took pictures for our IDs, and fingerprinted us for their investigation. We were told we would stay in the main building until their investigation was complete, and then they would decide where to send us. There were hostels for emigrants all over Austria. People stayed there for months waiting out the emigration process. We would have to wait too, and follow their decisions. We were completely in the hands of the Austrian government.

Now I know we were in the hands of God.

They took us upstairs to an isolated section of the building. To our surprise, they separated us. Daniela and I were placed in a room with families, while Attila was placed in the room for single men, because we were not married. We wanted to be together, but we had to follow their decisions, we had no choice. We were happy they accepted us. There were several rooms with twenty to fifty people from many different countries: Czechoslovakia, Hungary, Bulgaria, Poland, Romania, Yugoslavia and Turkey. We each received a heavy grey blanket, a small pillow, and an army-style aluminum container for food. We brought the container to the dining room for every meal, and then washed it and carried it back to the room with us. They also provided us with towels and toothpaste.

Daniela and I had bunk beds in the crowded room. I was afraid to leave Daniela alone in her bed. I slept next to her and held her tightly. I awoke often, unable to sleep most nights with the constant noise of conversation, crying, or snoring. We were locked within the building, limited to the room or the long hallway. We were not allowed outside. We spent most days walking the length of the hallway, waiting and talking about our unknown future. The weather was beautiful outside. Looking through the windows we saw golden-red autumn. I longed to be outside, in nature. But my duty in life was different, for the moment. For the next two weeks, we watched the leaves change colour from behind the glass.

Those two weeks in isolation felt like a lifetime. Every morning, we hoped to hear our names from the speakers in the hallway. Every time someone's name was called they left isolation and were sent to a hostel. We were aware that if they separated us from Attila here, they could also send us to different hostels. We could end up hundreds of kilometers apart. It was a difficult thing to acknowledge, but it could be our reality. We trusted. Soothed by moments of deep comfort, I knew all was well. The surprising challenges felt like a part of the process we needed to face. It was my truth I had chosen, it was my truth I lived. One day, while we were waiting in isolation, Attila looked at the map of Austria we had bought in Vienna the first day of our journey. He told me he hoped for a hostel near Mariazell, a town in the beautiful Alps. He had heard about it before. There was a big church that attracted people from all over. It was a pilgrimage town. I remembered my grandmother telling me about it. Observing the map, and dreaming about a beautiful place to go, felt much better than focusing on the unknown. The time to leave the camp would come, whether we waited with fear or not. It was easier to wait with trust and believe that the life we wanted was headed our way. We had little, but we had each other's support.

After two weeks in isolation, I surrendered to the waiting, making it through the days the best I could. I wished for a long hot shower, or a bath. I loved the feeling of my clean skin. Water soothed my Soul. There were only a few showers on the floor for almost two hundred people. If I could call it a shower; instead of shower heads there were pipes sticking out from the wall. There was always a line-up for a lukewarm or cold shower. I was lucky a couple of times to have a shower with hot water, around four o'clock in the morning. Weeks earlier, I would never have imagined this would be my life.

While we waited, we met many people. They told us why they emigrated and how they did it. Listening to their stories made me realize how blessed we were. There was a man who flew over the border in a hang-glider. A family we met at the ramp with two small boys had emigrated from Czechoslovakia through Yugoslavia. They had left their children with strangers in Yugoslavia, trusting these strangers to drive their children across the border, while they hiked through the mountains into Austria. Their story stunned me, their trust amazed me, and it was beyond my understanding.

Now I know that the power of knowing and faith creates everything we can imagine. That family now lives in Western Canada.

The morning of October 13 began as every other since our arrival in the camp. We got up, got dressed, and did a quick cleanup before a police officer unlocked the hallway door for us to go downstairs for breakfast as a group. That was the routine for each meal. Between meals, we were returned to the isolation floor, and locked in, where we only had access to the room with our beds and the hallway next to it. After returning to this floor, we walked the length of the hallway to pass time, patiently awaiting the voice on the loud speaker—hoping to hear our names called. Every morning they called the names of twenty people who were chosen to leave the camp. Unfortunately, some people lived there for a few months, waiting for the next formalities to take place.

Like all other mornings, the moment the officer started speaking everyone in the hallway fell silent. Hope on every face slowly evaporated as names were called and people realized it would not be their day. As the voice on the loud speaker called the names, I thought of how badly I wanted to leave this place. The names continued...not me, not Daniela, not Attila...the next names will be ours...the next names will be ours. My thoughts gained speed and my emotions followed. I acknowledged and discarded the reality that I had the same thoughts each morning, because today felt different. Today my hope was strong, because today was the thirteenth, and thirteen was my lucky number. Then suddenly, we heard our names, all three of them. Happiness flooded my being, my heart beat faster, and my blood rushed through my body. Everyone that was called today shared the same joy, the same relief, and the understanding of the disappointment of being left behind. We were leaving this forced insulation.

After weeks of being inside, we were free to go outdoors. First, we made a trip downstairs to get papers and identification cards. We did not get our passports. These would be returned only upon our leaving Austria. Today we would know which hostel would become our new temporary home. Standing in the line, I felt my body tighten. The question returned: What if we were separated? How would we work it out? We had to make it work somehow. We would. We wanted. We trusted. Our turn had finally arrived as we faced the lady in the small window. She would assign us to a hostel. To our pleasant surprise, she spoke Hungarian. Attila was Hungarian-born in Czechoslovakia. He understood—an amazing coincidence. He asked if she could send us to the same hostel. She said that she could. We were amazed again when we found out she had assigned us to a village in the mountains only six kilometers from Mariazell, the place Attila had pointed out on the map when we first arrived at the camp. It was a very happy moment for us. It was meant to be for us to journey together.

It did not matter to us that we had different names. It only mattered that we were going to the same address. Although we faced many challenges, the rewards felt great.

Looking back now, I know nothing was a coincidence. Everything in life happens for a reason, I believe. We were meant to be together. It was God's will. We had a destiny to complete.

Chapter Thirteen

Lucky number thirteen...

The light breeze on my face, after two weeks indoors, felt like a rebirth. The Austrian government accepted us as refugees. We did not have to return to Czechoslovakia. We were safe now, and shelter would be provided to us while the immigration paperwork was completed. We were given three destinations to choose from: Australia, Canada, or the United States. Without hesitation we chose Canada. Normally, the paperwork and permission to immigrate into another country took eight to twelve months. Wait times could be shorter or longer depending on the case. Our future was in the hands of the Canadian Embassy now, and I wondered about our unmarried status and whether it would have an impact on the length of our wait. But still, I trusted. Our dream was in motion while we waited our interview date to come.

The Guesthouse—hostel—was in the small town of Gusswerk. It was dark when we arrived and we saw little of our surroundings. But I will never forget the sense of peaceful beauty as we stood before the hostel for the first time, as though the whole world had opened up for us. The owner of our temporary home led us upstairs to our room. It had two windows with white curtains; three chairs surrounded a table covered by a perfectly ironed linen tablecloth. There were blue blankets on two twin beds, and a third, small bed by the window, for Daniela. Clean and cozy, the room invited us to stay. We were happy to be there, knowing we would stay until our papers were ready. It felt like home. In that moment, we had everything we could ask for. We had a clean comfortable place to stay, three meals a day, and most importantly—we were together. We were safe, with the emigration process in full swing. When our hostess left our room, we opened a window and stared in wonder at the shining stars in the night sky. Truly a magical night.

I opened my eyes the following morning, greeted by the sun shining through the curtains. Daniela slept peacefully in her bed. I wanted to see the scene from our room, so I peeked through the window. It was an amazing view with mountains surrounding us and a river with crystal clear water curving along the road. Nearby, I could see colourful stucco homes and a big creamy-coloured church with a black roof stood across the street, housing a school with a playground behind it. Everything looked clean and organized. Flowers bloomed in window boxes on every house. I felt blessed. I felt as though I was in a fairytale.

These are memories I love to go back to. The times when my life was testing me most, and at the same time life was giving me the most beautiful moments to remember and to cherish in my heart forever.

The Guesthouse was old, with at least ten rooms filled with families, single women, and single men from different countries. On the main floor was a restaurant with a big kitchen. After breakfast, we explored our new hometown. Fewer than a thousand people populated the small town, and still it offered all the necessary things, a variety of stores, a dentist, a doctor, a post office, a bank, and restaurants. The locals were friendly and welcoming to strangers. They were beautifully dressed in their Austrian regional attire. We also met some other residents of the hostel, who seemed genuinely pleased to meet us, and provided us with some useful information. We talked about the emigration process and found we understood each other. We shared the same feelings of uncertainty and hope.

With many families in the hostel, Daniela made friends. They were playing and learning together. Days passed, we had little to do, but it felt good to relax after a period of such uneasiness. Our stay in the hostel felt similar to a vacation. Each day we explored the beauty of nature surrounding us. I loved the time spent with Daniela and Attila as we awaited our interview, enjoying long walks in nature. We had time to get to know each other.

We wished to explore Austria, but we had no money for it. Occasionally we worked. Men often helped small companies with construction, painting, and gardening, while the women cleaned homes, or washed dishes in restaurants. We made some money, but it was very little. We also received a small monthly stipend from the government to help us. Even with these limitations and an unknown future, we had a great time. Our basic physical needs were met and we knew we were safe. We were grateful. Our life had become a waiting game, and we accepted our circumstances because we knew we would eventually find our way to Canada and a new life.

Months later, we celebrated our first Christmas in Austria. So very different from Christmases in the past; this one was without our family. We decorated a small tree and placed it on the table in our room. The three of us felt like a family. In this small hostel, we felt like one big family. We celebrated together. We knew another family from back home—we worked for the same company. They were staying in a hostel not too far from Gusswerk, and they visited us that evening. They had also chosen to immigrate to Canada.

The family now lives in Vancouver, British Columbia.

Daniela looked beautiful in the new Christmas outfit my uncle had sent from Canada—a white blouse and a black velvet skirt. I wore secondhand clothes from the Red Cross, because I had gained some weight and most of my clothes no longer fit. The escape from my unhappy life agreed with me, I was healthier and more relaxed. We enjoyed a peaceful evening in our cozy room, while snow softly fell, creating the perfect Christmas atmosphere.

It was a long, cold January. Some people from our hostel had their interviews, but the embassies reported that they were not accepted. When we heard this, we were stunned. We were naïve. It had not crossed our minds that the embassy could turn down our request. Every day we learned something new about emigration. Each case had its own nuances, so we could not make any comparisons. People applied to different countries, with or without sponsors; there were families, single people, and divorced people. There were those with different levels of education and knowledge of different languages.

The invitations for interviews from the Canadian embassy arrived. We had separate invitations on different dates. Attila had his interview first and was accepted by the Canadian government. We knew he would leave for Canada within the next six months. My interview was a few days later than Attila's. At the conclusion of my interview, the translator told me—while I was still in the office—that I was not accepted by the Canadian government. No explanation was provided. Shocked by the news, I left the large office closing the tall wooden door behind me. All I could do was cry. I did not know what to think. I was devastated, unable to say anything to Attila in the waiting room. But he knew.

We returned to our hostel, my mind was blank. How would we handle this situation? This question kept surfacing, and I could not hear the answer. I would never know their reason for turning us down, nor who made the decision. My only explanation was that perhaps it was because I was a single mother. The truth of the matter was that I had not expected being declined entry. Everything had become complicated. Our lives were no longer under our control. My life felt like a wild river, the water taking me wherever it wanted.

The complications were a consequence of the choices I had made. Consequences I must deal with, and I would. I would not give up the life I envisioned for us. I knew it awaited me. People empathized with me, and I received much support. They wanted to help, but there was not much anyone could do. It was my truth, my life to deal with—physically and emotionally. I could only hope, trust, and wait. The way for us to get to Canada was to get married, then I could go as Attila's wife, but getting married was not an immediate option because neither of us was divorced. Our divorce proceedings had just begun. There was nothing we could plan or predict for how the formalities of this emigration process would shape from then on. The only thing we knew was that we wanted to live together. We felt the bond of love between us. We wanted to share our life together.

Spring followed the snowy winter. Living in Austria for over five months, we found it to be a beautiful country: mountains, rivers, amazing nature coming alive again after winter. Because the days were growing longer, we spent more time outside. It seemed as though time passed more quickly with the spring even though there was not much we could do to help the process along. All we could do was keep hope alive. When June came around, we still had not received any news from home about our divorces. All our families could say was that our applications were in process. Again, more waiting. They promised to contact us when they had any news to provide. Our only certainty was more waiting.

Chapter Fourteen

My birthday in Austria...

Lucky thirteen. My first birthday away from home was greeted by a lovely morning. A year earlier, I celebrated my quarter century milestone with my parents and closest family. I wore the gold chain my parents bought me. The call to leave my birth country was too strong within me; but, when my birthday came I missed my family. I thought about them and how they felt about my leaving—I knew they understood my need to emigrate. I deeply felt the love we shared through our hearts even though we were not physically together.

I celebrated with my daughter and Attila. He was not yet my husband, nor my fiancé, but much more than a friend, although he was that too. We lived together for the past five months. I loved him, trusted him, and wanted to spend my life with him. I knew he felt the same. It was as though we had known each other forever. I sensed we were meant to live together and to learn from each other. We met so that we could share our journey, explore, love and grow together. This birthday celebration would be the first of many we would share. We had a long, beautiful journey ahead of us. We sensed it.

Our new friends in this new home, celebrated with us. I felt older than my twenty-six years given all the excitement and turmoil I had gone through in the last few years, and my daughter, six years old, would enter school in September. Whatever life brought my way, I always saw a bright future. I had faith. I knew life was amazing.

I enjoyed my day. After lunch we sat with a group of our friends and they wished me all the best for my birthday. We laughed, shared stories, and enjoyed each other company. Relaxed and happy, we were a big family feeling for each other and hoping for the best for each other; sharing the same feeling of being refugees.

I offered to make coffee and went to our room to prepare it, enjoying the feeling of my inner happiness. It was a beautiful afternoon. I was surrounded with big-hearted people; my little Daniela, Attila and all our friends. I placed the white porcelain cups with the freshly made coffee on the tray. I returned to the dining room, placed the tray on a table and realized everyone sat frozen in their spots. Nobody said a thing, something had happened in my absence. They stared, wide-eyed, Attila's eyes met with mine. I felt he wanted to say something, but he was totally silent. I felt Attila's tension and I wanted to know what happened when I was in the room preparing coffee.

What? What? What? The question resounded within my head as I observed everyone in the room and kept the smile on my face. What could possibly have happened in the ten minutes I was gone? Suddenly, the talking began and everyone rushed to finish their coffee. Something had happened and it was obvious no one wanted to discuss it.

Attila asked whether we could take Daniela for a walk. Confusion and curiosity washed over me. Just thirty minutes earlier we had been laughing and celebrating my birthday. Tension was in the air. Whatever happened in my absence completely stumped me. I did not know what to think. I took a moment to wash the cups in the room, then I put a light sweater over my shoulders, and off we went for our mysterious walk.

Usually, we walked into the mountains toward a house where they had goats. We would feed them bread and watch them run around. On that day, Attila led us to the woods by the creek. A fresh, vibrant meadow with colourful wild flowers greeted us, contrasting the tension in our bodies. We had only been there a few times before. The clear water in fast running creek offered a lovely, soothing soundtrack as we walked to the far end of the town, crossing the creek on a wooden bridge into the beautiful woods. Surrounded by tall trees with fresh green leaves, the sun shone through the foliage making it appear a magical place. It was late afternoon in mid-June, peaceful and quiet. I was glad I had chosen to bring my sweater as a chill stroked my body. I had enjoyed our lunch and was thinking about the strange way it had ended, and at that moment I experienced a shaky feeling in my body. I waited for Attila to say something with every step I took. Was there a surprise for me? It was my birthday.

Attila stopped and turned to me, then said, "I have to tell you something..." The shaky feeling intensified. Then he continued, "When you were in the room making coffee, a police officer came to tell me I am scheduled to fly to Canada on July 25th."

The words were like a knife in my stomach. I could not believe what I heard. My throat tightened and I could say nothing. There were no tears. I felt frozen. Even though both of us knew he would be leaving because he had been accepted by Canada, it was shocking news. When my brain kicked in again everything returned to me in slow motion. All that had happened that afternoon. Our friends had witnessed what I had not. It was why they were so still when I came back with the coffee. We stayed in that spot, hugging each other, all three of us. We knew we would handle this, silently, without words. We knew.

Attila would leave in six weeks and I would stay in Austria with Daniela. It was not how I had envisioned our future. My application to Canada was refused. We were not yet divorced, so we could not get married and all I knew was that I could not go to Canada with Attila. Again, all I could do was hope and wait. I wanted to believe that this challenge was the last one on my journey to Canada. What else could possibly come my way and sit so heavily upon my shoulders?

I held onto my faith. I knew the sun would come up after every dark night. With these thoughts in my mind, we slowly walked back to our temporary home, none of us knowing what to say. Dealing with our emotions was not easy. We knew we would be separated in six weeks with thousands of kilometers between us, but we did not know for how long. Daniela could not fully understand what was happening—she was too young, only six years old. She patiently walked with us, tightly holding our hands. That night I could not sleep; instead, I wondered how it all would fall into place. How would this dream of mine, of ours, come together? When would I go to Canada to join Attila, where we could live like a family, happily ever after? All I could do was pray. Finally, I slept.

The next day we called home and told our families the news. They wanted to visit before Attila left. Attila's mom and my parents managed to get papers. When someone emigrated, the government often granted the parents' permission to visit in hopes they could convince their children to return home. This would not happen in our case, and our parents knew that.

My uncle from Toronto, Canada made the trip to Austria so he could see my mother—his sister—after a forty-year separation. My mom was only ten when he left our country. He and his wife came to attend the World Congress of Youth taking place in Austria that year and could not pass up the chance for a reunion after so many years. We did not ask my uncle for sponsorship as it was a big responsibility and we were already in the process through the government program. It felt good just to know that there was a blood relative in Canada.

I was happy to see everyone at this special family event. It was great to see my mom and her brother reunited. We spent a few wonderful days together. My mom brought a Slovak national costume for little Daniela to wear for the reunion. It was my mother's costume, sewn by my grandmother when my mother was Daniela's age. More than forty years old, it remained in good condition. I remembered wearing that costume when I was little. My daughter looked so sweet in that white and blue costume. My mom made that reunion extra special for all of us. Together, we went to a big church in Mariazell and I felt gratitude for all of us being together again.

Soon, everyone left to return home and we were facing the reality of emigration again. We had only one more week to spend together in Austria with no news about our divorces on the horizon.

Chapter Fifteen

Time to say goodbye...

July 24, 1989 just minutes after 3:00 am, Attila and I stood outside in the parking lot in front of the hostel awaiting the bus that would take Attila away from us. He had to return to the refugee camp so he could obtain his landed-emigrant papers, his ticket for the flight, and his passport. He would stay there overnight and then get on the bus to the Vienna airport with everyone else the next day. Attila's final destination was Quebec City; he would land in Montreal, and then take a connecting flight. The Canadian Government had chosen the location for him, no explanation provided. He spoke no French, nor did he know anyone there, but he had to do as he was told.

While outside waiting for the bus, memories came back to me. Over nine months ago, we came to this parking lot after two weeks in isolation at the refugee camp, filled with happiness and a sense of freedom. We spent nine months, dreaming and planning our life together. And this morning we stood there again, looking into each other's eyes, saying nothing. Words could not describe our feelings. We silently promised each other we would do everything we possibly could to be together again. soon. We knew it could take a while. In that silence we heard the bus, then saw the lights approaching us from the darkness of the early morning. The emotion of the moment was strong; we knew it would stay with us for the rest of our lives. We hugged each other, holding tight, and told each other everything would be okay. We could do it. We would be together again soon. We knew there was no need to say more. Our feelings said everything words could not. The bus had arrived. We kissed each other.

There was no question about our love. We did not see this separation as a test of our love. We knew it would make our love stronger.

Attila boarded the bus. Through the windows, I watched him find a seat. We stared at each other through the window and waved as the door closed and the bus moved forward. I stood there alone, watching the bus disappear in the darkness. I cried quietly as I returned to our—my—room where Daniela peacefully slept. I crawled into my bed, feeling weak and cold. I needed rest and strength to deal with my life. Alone with my daughter, I fell asleep. My truth was a challenge I was willing to overcome.

Toward the end of July, I began thinking about Daniela starting school. We had a great time together. We walked almost every day through the woods, admiring the beauty of nature. Daniela would pick wild flowers for me, because she knew I loved having fresh flowers in the room. She was such a happy child, always sharing her loving heart with me and with everyone. She was always smiling and singing; joy poured out of her. I felt blessed with my angelic girl, even though everything was uncertain and complicated. I did the best I could for both of us.

August passed quickly, with no news from the lawyers back home. Our plan was to obtain our divorce papers as soon as possible and then get married. Only then could I join Attila in Canada. We had a clear plan, but we did not know when it would happen. Others were responsible for making decisions in our case. Time was unknown.

Chapter Sixteen

Big surprise...

In August, I received a phone call from my parents telling me my brother, Marian, was in a refugee camp in Austria. He emigrated with a friend from our town. My brother was single and had been living at home with my parents when I left. He had a good job and a great life at home. I was surprised that he left, but I was also happy knowing I had family here in Austria. Assigned to a hostel far from us, we did not see each other often but I felt our connection. Just knowing that he was in Austria, and we could see each other now, made me happy.

I often thought about our future life in Canada. My brother also applied to immigrate to Canada. He waited for his interview. Although Attila and my brother had met only a few times before we left the country, they both liked fixing cars and thought they might work together when we all lived in Canada. One day...

On a warm Saturday afternoon, my brother came to visit us. He was a fortunate emigrant, for he had a car. He took us to Mariazell. We toured around, visiting the well-known local church. Peace enveloped me whenever I was in that church. I felt the power of silence there—the power of prayer. I walked around feeling love, and was thankful for all the gifts in my life. I silently prayed for us to go to Canada, to start a new life I had imagined for so long. I strongly held my vision of the reunion with Attila in Canada. I never doubted that it would happen, and now my brother would live there too. The waiting, the not knowing when we would go to Canada was not always easy. I hoped we might be together for Christmas, which seemed so far away from summer time. Still, I saw my blessings and I was thankful for them. My brother was there and I had my daughter with me. We had a great afternoon together. We took pictures and created wonderful memories. It felt good to spend time together. We did not talk about emigration, or any of our issues. We just wanted to have a good time. After spending our day together, Marian took us back to the hostel and then returned to his.

Days passed, I was lucky to get a job in the kitchen of our hostel. I washed the dishes after lunch and dinner. Only a few hours, two to three times a week. Everyone tried to earn some extra money, so we shared the job in the kitchen. They paid little, but I was thankful for the extra money, and the job helped make time pass a little more quickly.

Chapter Seventeen

Time for Daniela to go to school...

September arrived, another new beginning for Daniela and me. She was excited to start grade one where she would learn how to speak, read and write in German. We got up early the morning of her first day and dressed in our best clothes. Daniela's enthusiasm made my heart sing. It felt like a celebration as we held hands on the walk to the school only a few minutes from our hostel. It reminded me of my first day of school in my hometown.

The school was old, small but clean and nicely organized. The teacher showed children where to sit. Daniela sat in the first row. I knew she was going to be an easy-going student. She was organized, responsible, and wise for her age. I never feared that she would cross the road without first checking for cars. She was also creative; she loved to make things with her hands. She loved and respected adults and children. She was outgoing, giving, and easily made friends. Daniela loved nature and animals, flowers and plants. She was a great child and that made my time alone with her much easier. She showed me only love. There was nothing, nothing at all, about my daughter that caused me any concern. I was a fortunate mother.

Daniela liked school. We confirmed she was left-handed, which did not surprise me; she often favored her left hand. I remember when I would hand her a spoon to eat with when she was little, and she took it with her left hand. She was a great little student. I did not have to tell her to do her homework. She took responsibility for her schoolwork, even at such a young age. She was happy to go to school every morning, and I really liked the educational system in Austria. It was a highly ethical approach, which taught children to be organized, to mind their manners, to respect others and to care about nature. They did not wear uniforms, but girls had to wear skirts or dresses. Daniela liked dressing up for school. They also used ink for writing instead of pencils, which reminded me of when I was in school.

Everything felt great. We had our daily responsibilities, but still had fun. Each morning I dropped Daniela off at school, and I went to work in the kitchen for a few hours, and then I walked back to school to meet her at the end of class. School finished at 12:30 pm, so we had lunch together and then went for a walk. Sometimes we hiked up the hill to see the goats and feed them. After our playtime, Daniela would do homework. I would join her at the table with my knitting or cross-stitching. She was so clever and studious that she did not need my help. I could not help her, because everything was in German and she was picking it up more quickly than I was. I would sit there and enjoy watching her passion for school. She often pretended to be a teacher for her teddy bears and dolls, who she gathered around her on the floor with her notebooks. Daniela was always so sweet. In her little pink dresses, skirts and sweaters she always looked girly even though I had cut her hair short. I loved cutting hair, I had been my family's hairdresser from the time I was fifteen years old. I believe I was born with this gift.

September was a beautiful time of year. The air was still warm and fresh breezes blew. Leaves started changing colours, reminding me that the end of the month would mark one year since we had left our country. Attila had been in Canada for the last two months. Two weeks after arriving in Quebec City, he had moved to Toronto and rented a small room in a house. He took English classes and was learning a new lifestyle in a new culture. We wrote to each other and only occasionally talked on the phone, because we could not afford the long distance charges. We missed each other and wanted to be together but life was showing us a different experience.

One day, after what seemed like a long wait, a phone call from home delivered good news: our divorces would soon be official. It meant our divorce papers should arrive within a few weeks. I called Attila to share the good news. He was as happy as I was. It was wonderful to hear his voice, to share the hope of being together soon. We could be married shortly and we hoped to be together for Christmas. We learned we could get married from a distance. To start the process, we would need to hire a lawyer; this meant more waiting. Only after we were married could Attila sponsor Daniela and me, which would take time. So, my hope of being in Canada with Attila for Christmas was a tiny flame knowing how much paperwork was involved. It was a lot to handle, but we knew we could do it. Nothing seemed impossible. We wanted to be together. We would be together. For Christmas, we hoped.

Our divorce papers came at the end of September. We could finally be married. Married...I kept repeating this word to let it sink it. After all the time we waited to be together, our dream of becoming husband and wife felt incredible.

Chapter Eighteen

Distance made our love stronger...

We took turns calling each other, unable to talk for long because the calls were expensive. We spoke about the next steps with each call. We found out it would not only cost a lot of money to hire lawyers to get married from a distance, but it would be a long process. This was not an option for us. We needed to find a different way. We could not lose our faith that there must be better solution. Attila talked to the people in the Canadian emigration office, who advised him we should marry in Austria. It would be a great cost for Attila to travel back to Austria, but it would be faster. It was hard to imagine how we would manage it, but we knew we had to act fast. We wanted to start to live our dream life in Canada together. Between the waiting and the many challenges, we managed the best we could while Attila prepared the paperwork and applied for our visas. He collected all the information regarding sponsorship. With all the new challenges and our limited money, we stuck to our plan because it was what we wanted. We kept our plan alive.

Attila saved some money from his small jobs after school, but it was not enough for this trip. A family who had moved to Toronto from our home country was kind enough to loan Attila the money to buy a plane ticket to Austria. He had met them only twice. It was an amazing act of love and understanding. There were great people everywhere in the world.

We are not in close contact with this family, but we are forever thankful to them. Their generosity means lot to us. It is one of the many great memories we deeply cherish.

Because of the big-hearted couple, Attila returned to Austria. We were blessed. Everything happened suddenly, after such a long time of waiting. We were excited that we were going to see each other again and would soon be married.

It took two weeks for Attila to receive his visa. We counted down the days until his arrival. Our dream was slowly coming true before our eyes. I planned what Daniela and I would wear on my wedding day. We had no money for new outfits, but I wanted us to look nice for this special day. I needed shoes as I had only walking shoes and running shoes. I had a lovely light-pink dress my mom had brought for me when she visited. I had worn it for previous special occasions, but left it home when I emigrated. Maybe my mom had a feeling I might need it. Daniela had the pretty white blouse and black velvet skirt she wore for our first Christmas in Austria. There would not be a large family celebration, but I was happy that my brother could attend our wedding ceremony.

On a beautiful sunny October day in 1989, Attila arrived. He rented a car in Germany and drove from there because it was less expensive to fly to Germany than directly to Austria. Attila parked the car in front of the hostel while I waited for him at the front door. We were happy to be reunited. Knowing it would take only a couple of weeks before were married was a beautiful feeling. Even through all the challenges we faced, we were thankful for all our blessings and it helped us to hold onto our visions and plans. The love in our hearts was—is—a strong force. It creates miracles.

Looking back, life presented many challenges and, at the same time, so many beautiful and meaningful moments. These meaningful moments would always stay with us, forever in our memories.

The day after Attila's arrival, we drove to Traiskirchen's City Hall, near the refugee camp. It was the only place we could get married, because we were not Austrian citizens. They gave us the next available appointment for the ceremony—October 31. Since Attila had to return to

Canada on November 5, the timing was perfect. I found the date interesting because I considered 13 to be my lucky number, and from that day on so was the number 31. Attila's birthday was also on the 31st but during the summer. There were numerical synchronicities in our birthdays and our wedding date.

We had more than one week to prepare for our wedding. I made myself a small bouquet. I love flowers and wanted pink roses to go with my dress. We bought one rose for Daniela. We also had to find someone who spoke German and Slovak to be our translator and witness. Our friends from back home who lived in a hostel not far from ours told us of a Slovak couple who spoke German. We had met them a few times before and we asked them if they would translate and witness our wedding. They agreed. Everything was falling into place for us. It was a magical time. All the formalities had been resolved. We were ready and happy for the day to arrive.

During our wait, we enjoyed every day together. It felt like our first vacation. We took day trips, exploring Austria, a beautiful part of the world. The beautiful natural scenery amazed us. Everything was the way it was meant to be. We counted our blessings. It was comforting to know we were surrounded with people who were willing to help us the best way they could with everything we needed. Where there is love, everything is possible

Chapter Nineteen

Our wedding day, this beautiful day is kept deeply in our hearts...

We were happy and everything was beautiful and meaningful on that special day. Our wedding was simple but magnificent at the same time. The Day was filled with love and a deep knowingness that our love would last forever. Our feelings were beyond words, I treasure them deeply.

Looking back now, more than twenty years, it was a part of the Divine Plan for us to be together. Love—God does not know obstacles. Anything is possible where there is faith. We were guided to leave our homes to live together, to fulfill our destiny together. Everything aligned for us to do so. Obstacles on our path were there to show us our strength.

We were blessed to have friends who gave us pictures of our wedding as a gift. We are thankful for the special gesture. It means so much to us. This couple now lives in the Toronto area. We are thankful for our witnesses and translators, who now live in Melbourne, Australia. You All made our wedding day special and beautiful. Thank you, my brother, for being part of the celebration of our love.

After 24 years of marriage, we still feel the great power of love we felt that day. We are as blessed and in love today as we were on our wedding day. There is no challenge in our marriage that our love cannot overcome. And that is Unconditional Love.

As I woke up I saw was my bouquet of pink roses on the table. Attila slept peacefully next to me, and Daniela looked relaxed in her deep sleep. We were married. We had four more days to spend together and then my husband would return to Canada while I stayed in Austria. I had to wait while the formalities were completed. We traveled to the Canadian embassy in Vienna to present our marriage certificate. The embassy would then send me an invitation for my medical check-up, something everyone had to complete before acceptance into their country of application. It usually took a few weeks to a couple of months. It is the end of October and I hoped everything would be done in time for us to get to Canada for Christmas.

We enjoyed our time in Vienna. Facing separation again in the next few days, we enjoyed every minute together. Daniela was always happy, smiling, looking cute without her front teeth. We toured the beautiful, historic city, and noticed that it felt different than the first time we came for our interview, almost a year ago. Then, we did not know what would happen. On this day, we did. We were applying to connect a family. We knew I would be going to Canada with Daniela. Since we were both healthy, it was just a matter of time. Time, we hoped, would pass quickly.

The day Attila had to return to Canada arrived. But this time, we were certain we would be together soon. This good-bye was much easier. In the same parking lot as a few months earlier, Attila put his suitcase in the trunk; we kissed and hugged each other with deep knowing that all was well and how we wanted it. We were grateful to be married and to know that we would be reunited in Canada soon. I watched him drive away, not moving from the spot until the car disappeared in the distance, again. We were separated, but this time was different. I returned to my room knowing everything was working for us. As always. Even when it did not look like things were working, they were, and I was ever thankful. I would soon fly to Canada with my daughter. We would be home soon. My new home, where I would live with my husband and daughter. How amazing.

Chapter Twenty

Life is ever changing...

Days were getting shorter and cooler. My daughter liked her school and had many new friends. Life was good as we waited to make our move to Canada. I found another job. It kept me busy and time was going faster. I worked in the mornings for a family that owned a small restaurant. The restaurant was attached to their house. I cleaned both their restaurant and their home—whatever needed to be done. It was a new building. Attila had occasionally helped with the cleaning while they were building the house when he was here in Austria. The owners were nice and treated me well. Their daughter, Michaela, was in Daniela's class. I was happy to have that job; it gave me something to do while Daniela was in school in the mornings. Days passed. I hoped the invitation for my medical exam would soon arrive.

Then something totally unexpected happened. An unpredictable challenge? On the morning of November 9, like any other morning, I went to work and Daniela went to school. When we later returned to the hostel, the other refugees were gathered in the dining room around the television. It was obvious something was going on because it was unusual to have that many people watching television during that time of day. I joined the others to watch the news program—the Berlin Wall was coming down. A revolution had begun. I sat stunned as I watched images of people and police on the streets of Berlin.

A few days later, revolutions erupted in Romania and in Czechoslovakia. My homeland would separate into two countries. I wondered about the chaos in the world. At least it happened peacefully in my country. People did not suffer as much as in other countries, and everyone in our families was okay. As I was never into politics, I did not understand why and how someone could create suffering for others. To me the separation of Czechs and Slovaks was not necessary. I believed in connecting not separating.

Suddenly, there was no reason to be a refugee anymore. With the border between our country and Austria opened, there was freedom to come and go between the two countries. There was freedom. We could go home. After being married for only nine days and my husband a landed immigrant in Canada we were suddenly free to go home. What timing. We were safe. We were lucky. I knew I would join him there. Our sponsorship papers were already with the Canadian Embassy. It was a blessing how things worked out just days before this widespread disturbance in Eastern Europe.

I wondered whether there was some unseen force that worked for us behind the scenes, simultaneously testing our strength. It was incredible how life took surprising turns.

Now I understand, in that chaos, everything was in perfect order—The Divine Order—and always is. It is much easier to go through all life's challenges with this awareness. Life always presents different challenges for us to see our strength and to grow. It is the purpose of life. The Soul grows through challenge, which does not necessarily mean suffering.

In this silent moment of realization, a question came to me. What would wander onto my path before I boarded the plane with Daniela on our way to join Attila? I had a sense everything would be okay. I would deal with everything that came my way, with all these political changes in Europe. Hope and faith never left me.

The emigration laws changed. Winter had arrived, promising the end of 1989. I was happy we were married, because the security of it helped me sleep at night. I did not have to worry that the emigration office would force me to leave the country now that the borders had been opened. It happened to those who were not accepted by their country of application. While I was waiting to go to Canada on sponsorship, others were being sent back home. We heard stories every day. There was nothing they could do. Some decided to stay in Austria illegally, but that posed its own risks. They would not obtain citizen status or support of any kind from the government. It was not easy witnessing the process for some of our new friends. It saddened me to imagine how upset people must have been, when they were forced to return home after planning a bright future in their "new home country." I had to believe their Divine plan was different and things would work out for them in different way.

A New Year—a new surprise, this time a pleasant one. The last day of 1989 came, and still I awaited the invitation for the medical examinations. We spent our second Christmas in the hostel in Austria, not together with Attila as I had hoped. The wait was longer than usual. After the medical exam, it would take another two to three months before I was granted permission to enter the country. I knew that meant if we got the invitation in January we would likely travel to Canada in April or May. At first a question kept repeating in my mind. How long a wait would I have? Only God knew. I felt part of my journey was to make peace with waiting. And I tried not to focus on how long it would take to move to our new home. Spring would mark a year-and-a-half for us in Austria. Not many people stayed that long. Most of the people we met upon arrival had since left for their new homes in Canada, the USA, or Australia.

New Year's Eve arrived and with it came great expectations for the New Year. Everyone in the hostel hoped 1990 would bring with it everything they hoped and dreamed. We all wanted new beginnings in our new homes. We all wanted our new lives to start.

We were dressed in our best clothes and enjoyed each other's company while we dined together in the hostel's dining room. Ignoring the hardships of the previous year, we were like one big family, sharing an understanding of our fears and hopes. We were on the same ship floating in the time of the unknown with one and the same destination in our mind's eye: A new home and new life. Near midnight, the champagne was poured while I wished my husband was there. It had been two months since our wedding and I missed him each day. Sometimes, I felt buried under heavy feelings stemming from waiting for so long and going through all these challenges. But I needed to continue my journey by allowing what was. I did not have many choices in the process. All I could do was just be, just go on the best I could. Midnight arrived. Happy people wished each other the best. High expectations for the New Year floated in the air—mirrored in everyone's eyes. My friends and I danced, chatted, celebrated, and had an all-around good time.

I could not help thinking about what Attila was doing in Canada. It would not be midnight there for a few hours. How was he celebrating New Year's Eve? Of course, these thoughts made me wonder how much longer we would be separated. The telephone rang again. Families from home called throughout the evening with their New Year's wishes. Someone called my name to tell me I had a phone call. I knew it was Attila. I was happy to hear his voice, and I was even happier to hear what he had to say. He told me he was returning to Austria for two months. He would join us and stay until we received our paperwork to enter Canada. We would fly to Canada together. Attila managed to save some money, and with winter in full swing his work had slowed, so he made the decision to visit us. He gave up his rented room and left his belongings with a friend. It was an amazing surprise. We hoped that we would return together, find a place to live and start our new life. In that moment, I felt close to him despite the thousands of kilometers separating us.

Again, we felt the stars in heaven aligned for us. A new year, a beautiful beginning. Love was ever powerful. We knew this would be our year, our beginning. This would be the year we would start our life in Canada together. Everything was working for us. We used our strength and our wisdom to go through our life tests. It felt right as it was.

Chapter Twenty-One

Beautiful winter in the Alps...

Although it was cold, it remained sunny. The mountains stood tall, showing their beauty. And the snow sparkled. It was magical when the sun set, and the stars and the moon introduced themselves. I felt peace and love within me. I watched the stars and dreamed. Love had no limits, love could make anything real. I trusted. I had faith. I loved. I saw. I knew. It was strong, pure, magical.

Now I know we feel love within when we fear nothing, when we trust. Love is powerful. It lasts. It creates. It helps overcome any challenge. It finds its way. It understands. Love is real. Only love is real.

I dreamed of Attila's arrival and how we would enjoy this winter together like we had the year before. Maybe we would build a snowman with Daniela. I could hardly wait for Attila's arrival. My brother offered to pick him up; together we traveled to the Vienna airport. I was happy to have my brother nearby. Although we did not see each other often, he was always ready and willing to help.

Our reunion was a happy one, and this time it looked as though we would travel to Canada together. That was our plan and hope. As the days stretched longer, we passed the time taking long walks, playing in the snow, and taking pictures with the small camera we bought. Every day we were amazed by the beautiful blue skies, white snow on the mountaintops in the distance, the cool dry air, and crystal clear water in the river. We sometimes fed the fish. There was much more to experience in the beautiful nature surrounding us.

Because the borders had been opened, we had many visitors. Attila's mom and my parents, our siblings and some friends, all came out to visit with us before we left. We had a great time. Even Daniela's father and grandmother came to visit and wished us a good life together. With all these visits, it seemed as though they understood, as though they forgave us for leaving. They loved us unconditionally and it was a great feeling. We were blessed to have our family. We had to follow our hearts, our calls and our life purpose. We could not do otherwise. It happened because it was meant to happen.

Now I understand that life is ever changing and with changes there are surprises that we need to learn to allow, and to deal with. Change is the only guarantee in life. When we allow change, life is much easier.

February arrived and still no invitation for the medicals. We had to allow what was. Attila would return to Canada in six weeks. There could still be a chance that everything would be completed before then. We knew miracles happened because we had already witnessed them. We trusted in the power working for us. We had been repeatedly challenged and discovered that if we refused to give up, we were rewarded. After everything I had experienced in the last year, I strongly believed in this. I could do nothing but hope and wish the invitation would arrive soon. I visualized it; I saw it in my hands. I believed the invitation would arrive any day, and it did, but we would not be going to Canada with Attila. We knew he would leave in two weeks and the exam results would come after he had left. The invitation was concrete evidence that our time in Austria was getting shorter.

We said good-bye to Attila for a third, and hopefully, last time. We knew our love was strong and real, and would overcome everything. Life was unfolding. Back in Canada, Attila found a better, steady job repairing cars. Meanwhile, Daniela and I were in the final stage of the medical exams. This was the last barrier to obtaining flights to Canada. The exams went well. I imagined packing our things. It was the end of March and I hoped we would leave for Canada within three months. I really wished to be there for my birthday in June. By that time, it would be more than one year since Attila learned he had been accepted into Canada. I was ready. I had had enough of waiting. I was ready.

Attila wrote that he had found a one-bedroom apartment and was preparing our new nest in Canada. He painted all the walls white and trimmed the doors and windows in light grey. He was on the search for simple furniture and comfortable beds. The apartment sounded wonderful. Attila told me it was on the seventeenth floor in a nice neighborhood in Etobicoke, outside of Toronto. In the far distance, he could see Lake Ontario. I was happy for us reading his letter, I felt like I was there with him. It helped make the waiting easier.

One day, my brother called with surprising news. He said that he received a letter from the Canadian Immigration Office—they had halted his application because the border to Slovakia had opened. As a result, he could no longer stay in Austria as a refugee. He had to return home. I was stunned. I had hoped he would immigrate to Canada with us. I did not know what to say. I felt his pain because I could easily imagine myself in the exact situation. Listening to him was all I could do to support him. Although he remained calm and said he understood why this was happening I could hear the disappointment in his voice. He would return home. He could stay illegally, but that was not like my brother. He had a job for the summer and his boss had offered him a room, so he decided to stay for the rest of the season without any status. I wished him the best. There was little else I could do. Our parents had not yet been told. He would tell them later. I was certain they would be happy and would support him emotionally when he returned.

Now, I question whether God sent him to Austria just for us. My brother had come when Attila left for Canada, and he returned home just as we were leaving. I questioned why this had happened. Was he there so we would not feel alone? Was he there as our Earth Angel? My brother has a big heart. He loves people and he always serves any way he possibly can.

Was I able to handle more challenges? I had no other choice. There was no giving up. Days passed. I still worked weekday mornings while Daniela attended school. The only difference was that the days were getting longer, and the snow was melting. Spring had arrived. It was a new beginning, signaled by nature, demonstrating the cycle of life. This was my second winter in Austria. I loved the country and the people, but Canada called me. It felt like the place I belonged, even though I had never been. That land called my Soul. I eyed my suitcases, almost packed, ready in the corner of our room. It had been over two months since our medical tests, and the wait seemed too long already. I was emotionally exhausted. I knew the envelope would arrive in the coming days and I was eager to know the date of our flight to Canada.

When the letter from immigration arrived, I felt every cell of my body dance with happiness. I was more than ready to see the flight date was finally within my reach. I felt so happy that I wanted to laugh and cry at the same time. I took the envelope and ran upstairs to go to my room. I wanted to open it alone to fully experience the joy of that moment. I, alone, understood the pain and disappointments I felt during my waiting process. I was excited about calling Attila to let him know Daniela and I would soon be with him. I planned to share the news with Daniela the minute she arrived home from school. This was going to be a moment I would never forget—the date of my flight, the day when I was finally ready to move to Canada. Finally, it was time to go home. All these thoughts and feelings fired like lightning as I was on the way to my room with the envelope in my hands.

I sat on my bed, tore open the envelope and almost fainted. On the third pass of the letter, I still could not believe my eyes. The letter stated—with apologies—that the paperwork from my medical exam was lost. I needed to restart the process and I also had to pay for the exam since I was being sponsored by my husband and not by the Canadian government. I imagined myself screaming as loud as I could. My body collapsed safely on my bed and I cried. Out loud I asked, "How much more could I handle?" It was the end of May. I knew I would not be with my husband for my birthday, which was two weeks away. The process could take three more months. I looked at the suitcases and surrendered…I had no choice…I had no choice…I had longer to wait.

As I lay on my bed, my muscles felt stiff and my mind continued spinning. My truth, in that moment, felt heavy. My mind gave no answers to why this was happening. All I heard was: you will make it through this, you are strong. I channeled my reserves and stood up. It was time to walk to school. Daniela was waiting for me. Thank God I had my daughter. She was a blessing in my life, and I had to be there for her. I wanted to be there for her as she was always there for me. Yes, this larger-than-life Soul in the body of an innocent child played a big role in my life. She was love; she was everything for me during these challenging times. I made peace with this situation. The truth was that I was lucky to have my part time job and the extra money to pay for medical exams.

My birthday came. I received postcards from Attila and my family back home. As much as I had to leave my country, I would always call it home. The postcards were a sweet reminder of love on my birthday. I also received a letter from the Austrian government—not a birthday wish. It was a notice that I had to leave the country, as they could no longer keep me as a refugee even though I was in the process of waiting to get my final papers and the flight date. It did not shock me as much as the letter about my lost medical papers. After all the challenges, and the last letter, I felt I could handle anything. I felt as though nothing could ever surprise me enough that I could not face it. I felt my strength and my willingness to face anything. And I knew there must be a different way to handle this than by going home. As I reread the letter, I made my decision: I would not go back to Slovakia. I would wait in Austria, somewhere. There must be a place for me and Daniela to stay while we awaited our flight. I could not picture myself going back. I would stay in Austria. I believed that was my truth. It was the decision I made and I was not going to alter it. I took one day at a time as my life unfolded with more challenges. I felt my strength.

The owner of the hostel received notice that we could no longer stay. Her compassion was great. She allowed me to stay, because I had a young daughter and she knew I would eventually fly to Canada. Because I was no longer considered a refugee, the government would no longer pay her for my lodgings. She asked me to work in the kitchen in exchange for our food and lodging. I always believed in the inherent goodness of people. I was amazed and thankful. Every challenge that I chose to accept with faith, to not give up, always resulted in a reward. I presumed she felt my desire not to return to Slovakia, because I did not tell her before she made her offer. The situation became easier to handle than I would have imagined.

How this Universe took care of me at that time, I only realized many years later. Only now do I see it clearly, what my Soul chose to grow through.

We stayed in the hostel. I kept my morning job while working in the kitchen. I appreciated the kitchen work and learned new cooking skills. As I settled into my new routine, I got the news I had to leave within two weeks, because the hostel owner had received notice from the Immigration Office that a new family would be coming. She needed our room for them. She offered to help in finding somewhere else for us to stay. Clearly, she wanted to help me; however, there was no guarantee she would find something for us.

I was blessed with many friends who wanted to help us. Feeling for us, they followed up with all their contacts to try to help find us a place to stay. I also asked the lady I was working for at my morning job, but she did not know anyone who could help me. With one more week to find a place, I felt overwhelmed. I could not help but wonder: Why me? Where would we stay until the final papers arrived? I packed the suitcases again, knowing we must leave even though I knew not where we would go. I held the vision and kept faith we would stay in Austria, because I wanted to stay in Austria.

People help because they love. Just days before we planned on leaving the hostel, a friend found a place for us to stay. My faith was rewarded yet again. A few kilometers away, in the mountains, a family owned a farm and a small restaurant. They rented rooms in their house during the summer when families from the city traveled to the mountains to find peace and quiet. Many of the guests came from Vienna. The family needed someone to help in the kitchen, to clean the guest rooms and for general help around the farm. They offered me this position based on my friend's request. Every cell of my body danced with happiness to hear the news. I was thankful and excited to find a way to stay in Austria. The family had three children who attended the same school as Daniela, and their mother could drive all the kids to school come September. It worked out better than I could possibly have dreamed. I hoped to leave the country before Daniela returned to school. The beginning of September would mark three months since my second medical exam. At that point, I counted not only months and weeks, but days.

Our two suitcases—now packed and waiting by the door of our room signaled another new beginning. I had never met the family we would live with and was excited for the day we were to meet. I trusted the unknown. It felt right.

We were ready to go. Nostalgia overtook me as I looked around. We had created wonderful memories to take with us. So many memories were created in this room, in this hostel, in this country. I had carefully packed my wedding bouquet—dried and preserved—to take to Canada; a reminder of the good times in Austria. I loved the time I spent with Daniela, Attila, and all the people, but I was ready to move on...I was more than ready. I watched from my bedroom window as a car pulled up to take us to our new home. A lady, who looked a little older than me, got out of the car and greeted the hostel owner with a hug. It was easy to see they already knew each other.

Daniela and I joined them outside and made our introductions. Elizabeth, my new employer and the owner of our new home, seemed genuinely happy to meet us. We said our good-byes, knowing we were leaving this place forever. We drove to the end of town and then up into the hills. With the sun shining through the forest of tall trees, I felt welcomed. The narrow road was not paved and we passed no other cars as we continued higher and higher into the hills. It was a dry, hot July afternoon and I could smell the evergreens through the open window. I felt as though we were on vacation. I welcomed the feelings of expansion. Daniela was happy; she was coping incredibly well with all these changes. I told myself that everything would be okay even though we had to be careful as we no longer had medical coverage in Austria. We were completely on our own, responsible for everything. Sometimes in life we have to take risks. It felt right. I trusted my gut feelings.

Chapter Twenty-Two

Another temporary home...

After a short drive, we came upon an open field with two large buildings, one their house–with a restaurant and rental rooms—and the other the barn. They had cows, sheep, and horses. The property was beautiful. I felt like we arrived in heaven, with the open sky, freshly cut grass, wild flowers blooming at the edges of the property, and a tiny chapel with a statue of the Virgin Mary on top of the hill. As the surroundings welcomed us, so did the family. Their grandmother—Oma, had grown up in the house. It had been passed down to her son and his wife, who were raising their family in the home. Greeted as though we were long lost family, it was an amazing experience. Daniela ran off into the fields with the children before the suitcases had been removed from the car. I was again thankful and so happy to see what I saw everywhere my eyes looked.

The owner of the house told me what was expected of me in exchange for lodging and food. I would work for them every day, with a break for lunch, doing anything that needed doing. They would also pay me a small amount so I could have some pocket money. Again, I received everything I could possibly ask for in my situation. I was happy to be there with Daniela. It seemed like a great place to live, and a great adventure.

After dinner we retired to our new room; a small room with two wooden framed windows. It was fresh and inviting—comfortable, like home. We were blessed, surrounded by loving people. When I turned off the lamp at night, the room was thrown into complete darkness. There were no streetlights here. The quiet was absolute. A gentle breeze blew through the open window, bringing with it the sweet smell of wild flowers. I felt at peace next to Daniela. Holding her tiny hand, I fell asleep happy in the knowledge we had a roof over our heads, food to eat, a warm comfortable bed, and acceptance by a loving family. The family had two boys, and a girl close to Daniela's age. They ran in the fields together. I loved seeing all four of them so happy and laughing, having good times together. I worked most of the day and had little time to spend with my daughter, but still she enjoyed her summer off with her new friends.

Many years later, Daniela told me that summer, living on the farm in Austria, was a great time. And I understand why. Not only were our earthly needs met, but the big hearts of that family helped meet our emotional needs. When we returned to Europe to visit our family after living in Canada for a few years, we also visited that family in Austria. I wanted my husband to know this family. It was a nice reunion. They welcomed us with their big hearts yet again, Attila included.

My life in our temporary home was not boring. I helped in the kitchen, doing laundry, cleaning rooms, and serving guests in the restaurant. I cleaned the machine used to milk cows and even helped with shearing the sheep. Some days I was tired, so I napped during my lunch break. Afraid I might sleep too deeply, I set my alarm clock. I never worried about Daniela, because I knew she was safe playing with the other children. Sometimes she would come upstairs and nap with me. I cherished those moments of togetherness. Every day before my afternoon shift, I received a treat from Oma. She greeted me with a smile, fresh coffee and a piece of cake or a pie she had baked. I was an employee, yet she treated me as family, reinforcing the inherent good that resided in people. She offered unconditional love to a stranger. I was constantly amazed by her giving heart. She was such a sweet Oma. We ate together, as a family, the food Oma prepared. These kind-hearted people demonstrated their thanks to God and life each day with giving thanks for each meal. While I was growing up, prayer was said in church or reserved for special occasions, like Christmas. While my parents always reminded us to be thankful for food, God's gift, grace was not performed before every meal. I considered this ritual a special reminder to be thankful for our gifts from Mother Earth. It warmed my heart with love and appreciation for the gifts of God at the table. The family lived a simple life, yet they were happy. They held a deep understanding of life, loving God and people, and knowing God and others loved them. I was thankful for the experience.

As August came to its conclusion and Attila's birthday arrived, I wished I could have celebrated his birthday with him in Canada. Nothing had come from the immigration office either. I waited for their letter with a quiet hope in my heart. My brother returned home to live with my parents. He had made good connections with people in Austria. The man my brother had worked for as a painter liked him and offered him a job for the future. They were painting big buildings, restaurants, and churches. He asked my brother to get a working visa, because it was too risky to have an employee without legal papers. So, my brother obtained a visa, lived with our parents and commuted to Austria for work. My brother was not only a good man, but also a handyman. I was happy for him. In the end, everything fell into place for him. He seemed happy to go back home and to work in Austria.

Twenty-five years later, my brother still works in Austria and lives back home in Slovakia.

I had hoped Daniela and I would travel to Canada before the school year began, but had not yet received anything from the emigration office. Daniela was happy to see her classmates again, oblivious to my desire to leave Austria. As we had lived in the mountains for the entire summer, she had not seen any of them. As agreed, Elizabeth drove all the kids to school. On a fresh September morning, I cleaned the rooms after the guests had returned to Vienna. I realized it would be two years since we emigrated. Two years and still we waited. The thought no longer made me uneasy. I had made peace with the waiting process. All was well.

While I would have rather been in Canada with my husband, this was my reality. I made the best of the situation. I was thankful for what I had.

One beautiful sunny day, at lunchtime, I made my way toward the small chapel on the top of the hill. I stood there, looking at the statue of the Virgin Mary. I closed my eyes, and took a deep breath of the flower-scented air as peace completely filled my being. I acknowledged my love for that place, those people, and their help on my journey. But I was ready to leave, ready to join my husband, ready to create our new life. I sent out these thoughts, the feelings strong within me.

I was given what I asked for. A few days later, I received a letter from Immigration. Having no expectations of the information contained within, I opened it. Everything had come together, we passed our medical exams, and our sponsorship was accepted. Oh, God Thank You. I breathed deeply as my eyes watered, joy filled me, and I was thankful–quietly, within my heart. The date was decided. We would leave from the Vienna airport on October 9, 1990. We would be in Canada that same day.

I called Attila. We were happy our reunion was finally on the horizon. Words could not describe our hearts' connection, our love stronger than ever. Attila paid for the tickets that would take us from Vienna to Zurich to Toronto. I would handle getting bus tickets, and booking a hotel in Vienna so that we would make our morning flight. After everything I had lived through, this would be simple…OH MY GOD, THANK YOU, THANK YOU. OCTOBER 9 WOULD BE THE DAY.

The day after my good news, I served coffee to new guests that had arrived from Vienna. One of the guests sat at the table as Daniela came in and spoke to me in Slovak. After my daughter left to play with the other children, this lady asked what language she had spoken. I told her, and she was surprised to learn Daniela was my daughter, she had presumed she was a sibling to the other children. She shared with me that her mother was Czech and that she understood some words my daughter had said. I spoke German with her. I was not fluent, but still she understood me. She asked about my immigration process, seeming interested. I was happy to share the short version of the process. I felt happy to share my news that we would be leaving Austria shortly. She seemed happy to hear it too. She then asked if we had somewhere to stay the night prior to our flight, because she knew that we would be staying in Vienna the night before the flight. This lovely lady (I now see her as an Earth Angel) offered to pick us up from the bus station in Vienna and let us stay overnight in her apartment. She then offered to drop us off at the bus depot the following morning. She wanted nothing in return. Her kindness was genuine and warmed my heart. Again, surprised by someone's generous act, I had no words other than–Thank You. Prior to her departure, she and the owner organized the timing and sorted out our bus tickets.

Even though we spent over two years in Austria and had many challenges and surprises, I felt fortunate and blessed. I would take many beautiful memories from the last two years, memories that would last the rest of my life. My dreams were slowly unfolding before me, I was feeling stronger than ever, and at peace. I packed our suitcases. Everything was in order, the path clear. We would leave tomorrow. For the last time, I called Attila. He told me he had a surprise for me. After the phone call, I walked up the hill to the small chapel. There I looked up to the sky full of bright stars and projected my profound gratitude.

Chapter Twenty-Three

Last few days in Austria...

We said good-bye to our extended family, hugging each other, knowing that we would one day see each other again. Sitting on the bus, I enjoyed the view as it passed our window. Beautiful Austria, for many reasons deeper than its surface. I observed the amazing scenery of its nature. Mountains, trees, flowers and rivers; it was as beautiful and majestic as that first day. Even after two years living in Austria, the views remained breathtaking. I felt as though I was flying. I closed my eyes for a moment, anticipating our arrival in Canada, savoring the reality that I would be with Attila the following evening. The time had come. It was my truth. I wondered about the surprise Attila had mentioned.

An image of being on the bus to Yugoslavia came to life in my head. July 1987, my first attempt at this journey. I was finally on the bus to the airport, finally going to Canada. It took over three years. In October 1990 I acknowledged how I had never let go of my dream.

In Vienna, our Earth Angel awaited us. She brought us to her apartment in the center of Vienna, easily accepting us into her home. She lived on her own and I wanted to pay her for our stay, but she refused my money. I noticed the common thread of generosity of the people I attracted into my life. All of them were loving and giving. Again, I was grateful. As promised, the next morning she dropped us off at the bus stop to catch the bus that would take us to the airport. She offered one last smile and wished us a safe trip and a great life in Canada. I watched as her car disappeared on the busy Vienna Street.

As I write this I remember that after a few weeks of living in Canada I sent her a postcard, wanting to keep in touch with her. I hoped to one day return her generosity. She never wrote me back. I believe it was not important to her and I accepted it. She was happy to serve us without any return. Her help and kindness meant a lot to me. I never forgot that feeling of gratitude. Looking back, I realize I was always blessed with people helping me on my journey while I was alone with my young child. I realized there are many Earth Angels ready to serve when we trust and allow. I was fortunate to know many of them during my journey in Austria.

Chapter Twenty-Four

The amazing feeling of going home...

At the Vienna airport, Daniela looked happy and beautiful as always. She looked cute in her new blue jeans and pink sweater. She looked grown up for her seven and a half years. It was a special day for us. We were going home, although I had never been to Canada it still felt like going home. With my papers in hand; the landed emigrant document, my passport, and tickets to Toronto, it felt right. In a short twelve hours we would be in our apartment. I could start creating my life in the country I had a call to live in since I was a teenager. The time between then and now seemed to span a lifetime. I felt such strength within me, because I never gave up my dream. I kept going and trusting my feelings that everything was and would be okay. It was.

I looked at Daniela and our two suitcases, wanting to call Attila one more time, just for a few minutes to share my joy. But it was early in Toronto, only three a.m. I would call him from Zurich, and assure him we were on our way, even though he already knew this. I wanted to hear his voice before I saw him that night. Instead, I let the feelings of peace, satisfaction, and gratitude float around my body. Stepping out of the emigration box, I would finally be myself again and make my own decisions rather than following others' decisions on my behalf. Although I was grateful for this experience, I was happy to move on and knew without it I would not be where I was at that moment.

We boarded, surrounded by many other emigrants. Recognition was simple; most carried old suitcases, others carried only boxes. I heard many different languages. For many, this would be their first flight, and a life-altering trip. Flooded by many feelings as I boarded the plane, I reminded myself that everything was okay and that it was normal to feel mixed emotions. This flight would alter the course of my life. Seated, we awaited departure. We sat in the middle rows and I wished we had window seats so that we could see the earth from above. The airplane started moving, faster and faster. We were leaving Austria, and it felt a lot like leaving home. This country, and the memory of my life there, would always stay deeply in my heart. It had strongly shaped me. The experience of my life there had shaken my core and, at the same time, showed me the deepest love and understanding of the human heart. On a deep breath, I took Daniela's hand in mine. She offered a bright smile. My little Angel, her presence supported me the last two years.

We landed in Zurich, Switzerland for the connecting flight to Toronto. I called Attila, and felt reassured by the sound of his voice and that each passing hour brought us closer together. Life was filled with rewards. I would shortly explore life in a new country with my husband. We would be together for our first anniversary, at the end of the month. I loved my life.

Once onboard our second plane, a much bigger one than the first, I considered my life in Canada. Although I understood little English and did not know what was ahead of me, I still expected it to feel like home the moment I stepped off of the plane. The strongest call in my life, my reality, my truth, was coming to life bit by bit. My inner voice made me strong, and it helped me to handle everything that came my way. That same voice had guided me and told me to have faith. My inner voice felt so strong that I could not do anything but follow my dream. I did it with passion and love.

As the plane began to pull away, I closed my eyes for a moment and smiled. That smile radiated throughout my whole body, within my very essence. I wanted to laugh out loud. I wanted to throw my arms in the air and celebrate. I wanted to hug everyone on the plane. I wanted to hug the whole world. I wanted everyone to feel the joy I felt at that moment. Instead, I silently celebrated the moment with my daughter as she was falling asleep next to me.

I woke up to the smell of food. It smelled delicious and I was hungry. We were flying over the Atlantic Ocean and Daniela was wide-awake, her cheeks pink and her smile happy. She always offered happiness and unconditional love. I considered her a blessing in my life. A young flight attendant, not Oma, served our lunch, and as I ate, memories of the last few weeks returned to me mixed with thoughts of my future. I wondered about the life ahead of me. Everything would be different. I felt as though I was no longer waiting for anything. I knew I would be in Toronto in five hours. I knew I would be in charge of my life from now on. I finished my coffee while I observed my surroundings. I was fascinated by the size of the airplane because I had once flown to Bulgaria and that airplane was much smaller.

I looked through the magazine in the seat pocket in front of me, I tried to read it, but I understood few words. Would I ever understand English the way I did Slovak? I knew I would learn some eventually—just as I had learned enough German to get around. But I did not write or read German. Daniela's grade two German was better than mine, but I was willing to learn. I wanted to know English the best I could. I slid the magazine back into the seat pocket. Daniela had fallen asleep and I wanted to sleep too. I had slept lightly the last few nights, because I was excited about this flight; a flight I had waited so long for. I closed my eyes to rest and thought that by the time I woke up we would be home in Canada. How amazing.

I had experienced many beautiful moments in my life, such as giving birth, and getting married, and that specific moment on the plane, I would remember alongside the others. In the air, I touched my daughter's hand, feeling the vastness of my heart, happiness and gratitude. I closed my eyes, surrendering to the fullness of life. I silently said farewell to Europe, the land where I was born, to my loving parents, my siblings, my friends, everyone I knew there, and the beautiful places in High Tatras, Slovakia, where I attended summer camps as a child. So many feelings of love and beauty struck my body in a split second. I drifted away from my conscious mind. Sleepy, I was at peace, again grateful and appreciating my life and all it had to offer. I was ready to receive it all. I imagined I had grown wings and was flying as I drifted off to sleep.

Suddenly, my body rocked from side to side rousing me from my drowsy state. I opened my eyes, wondering what had happened. Then it happened again. This second sudden movement awoke Daniela. She fumbled for my hand and silently we stared at each other. A man's voice came over the speakers, but I could not understand the message. The flight attendants came around checking everyone's seat belts as the plane continued shaking. The rocking increased. The man's voice again spoke. Again, I did not understand. I saw lightning through the windows and realized we were flying through a storm. The airplane continued shaking, unsettling the passengers. When the lights went off, people got loud until the plane started violently rocking. Then we sat in silence surrounded by darkness. I held tightly to Daniela's hand, my heartbeat increasing its pace, my stomach and throat tightening. The lights flickered as the plane continued its roller coaster ride. People were looking at each other with fear in their eyes. Flight attendants talked to people, but I could not understand what they said.

My heart was nearly beating out of my chest. I had never felt so scared. Ever. The captain's voice filtered overhead again, but the only word I recognized was emergency. This scared me more than not knowing what he was saying. The heavy turbulence continued and seemed to last forever. There was nothing I could do but hold Daniela close and pray to God. Daniela complained her ears hurt. She looked uncomfortable, but I could do nothing to help. I tried comforting her while she cried and lightening lit up the dark sky. All I could do was pray and trust everything would work out. In a moment of despair I feared we would die, and my body tensed. The turbulence grew stronger. Caught up in my fear, I lost track of time. I felt I had no choice but to make peace with this situation in spite of my fear. I had no power to control this. Whatever happened would happen. It was God's will. Deep within, I never lost hope that God's will was to get us to the airport where my husband awaited our arrival. Never so scared in my life, I shook inside not ready to die, and that was the thought bouncing around my head. In the depth of my Soul I was not afraid of death but I wanted to live, to experience all life had to offer. I wanted to live my dreams. Daniela had just started her life. We had sacrificed much for our new life, I begged God to get us home safely. Again my faith was tested. Daniela was terrified; we all were. I continued hoping all would be all right. Finally, we made an emergency landing in Halifax, Canada. We were not going to continue the flight to Toronto. I had wanted badly to touch the ground and was instantly relieved when the plane was again on solid ground; my body relaxed. Daniela's ear was sore, but she was no longer afraid.

The plane slowly lumbered forward and then suddenly stopped, the motors fell silent, as silent as the passengers. The captain's voice crackled above us, but I still understood nothing. We waited on the plane for the next steps. I had no idea how long we would be in Halifax and as much as I wanted to be in Toronto, I did not wish to fly again. I had to believe this was the last challenge on my journey to Canada. It must be. Images of what could possibly happen flashed through my mind, but I shut down the imagery, focusing instead on the fact that we were safe and would be home soon.

Four hours later, I fought to stay awake, wondering when we would leave Halifax. I knew we were only two hours away from our destination and really just wanted to be home. Finally, I heard the rumble of the motors and although I was—mentally and physically—exhausted, I was not too tired to be afraid. I kept telling myself everything was okay.

After an uneventful first half hour, Daniela and I finally slept. When I opened my eyes, I saw twinkling lights through the windows. We were close. The captain uttered more words I could not understand. But I knew, I just knew we were finally in Toronto. We are home was a litany in my head. I recognized the words Toronto International Airport. Everyone looked tired and many were not coping well with this delay. Not knowing what the captain or the flight attendants said, I held Daniela's hand and our bags as we slowly walked off the plane into a building where we had to wait.

We were tired and wanted nothing more than to sleep. But then the reality of our situation sunk in, Attila was close. We would be together soon. Suddenly fully awake, I waited for the reunion with undisguised joy. It had been six months since we last saw each other. The anticipation blossomed inside me as we were taken into a small office where they checked our papers. I understood the question: Who is waiting? And I knew to respond: my husband. Soon after, they let us go instructing us to follow the crowd toward the exit.

I searched the crowd, and then our eyes met. My heart beat quickly. I was humbled by the moment—we were finally together. Soon we would truly be home. I would never forget this moment. This was the moment we worked so hard to achieve. We had envisioned the beginning of our new life together in Canada for such a long time. It was a moment of pure love and understanding we held deeply in our hearts. This instant called to mind the first time our eyes met in this lifetime. The knowingness that we were meant to be together was unmistakable–we had a destiny to complete.

Chapter Twenty-Five

Finally coming home...

Attila unlocked the door to our apartment, welcoming us home. It was beautiful, clean, bright, simply furnished, organized, cozy, and inviting. I felt completely at ease. I recognized touches of love everywhere, Attila's happiness at preparing our new home evident in every room. I truly felt his happiness, which only served to increase mine. I felt tired after our long, challenging flight, but I desired to fully live this beautiful moment of coming home.

Near midnight, Daniela slept soundly in her new bed. My sweet little girl had handled so much in her short life—always with love. She would always be my sweet little girl, angelic in her white-pink pajamas.

I enjoyed a long shower, loving the simple luxury. I allowed the water to relax my body and wash away the feelings of fear and uncertainty. The emigration process was over. Oh, God thank you. I sensed expansion and love in my heart, encouraged it to grow. Being home with my loved ones was an incomparable feeling. I loved everything about that moment.

I checked on Daniela once again, loving how relaxed she looked in sleep. My body clearly let me know it was time to sleep. It was time to put the day behind me. As I lay down, with Attila for the first time in our new home, I marveled at the feel of the bed never having experienced it before. It was the surprise Attila had told me he had for me, it was a waterbed. I had never heard of such a thing. I was thankful for everything Attila prepared for us. Love was-is such a powerful creative force. I fell asleep in my husband's arms surrounded by love and filled with a true appreciation for life and all the sweet gifts it had to offer— my husband, my daughter, a cozy place to live, and beautiful Canada, a wonderful country to explore in this lifetime. Thank you, God...Thank you, God. I am home, I feel home.

THANK YOU.

Chapter Twenty-Six

September 2013 was twenty-five years since we left our home country of Slovakia, our place of birth.

Looking back, I understand why things happened the way they did. I see my past through the eyes of love. I am forever thankful to my loving husband for everything he did for us. I am thankful for being the mother to my beautiful daughter Daniela. And I am thankful for being who I am and the life I have in Canada.

The challenges of my life did not stop when I arrived. I left behind challenges that served their purpose, while life brought me different ones. I had to learn a new language. I had to adapt to a different culture, find a job, and many other challenges that came my way. I am proud as I look back at my life, knowing all the experiences—those I liked and those I did not—made me who I am today. As my life unfolded I learned how to categorize less—not at all—what I like and do not like. I found out life is much easier that way. I learned there is no right or wrong path to live. I learned how to create more of what I prefer and accept what I have no control over. I learned to see everything through the eyes of love. I learned to take responsibility for every experience in my life without blaming others. I learned that freedom and happiness is a state of being and it does not come by moving to a different continent of the world. I came to understand that everything I experience in my life, I create for the purpose of expansion. I learned that life itself is precious and incredible no matter what is going on. I learned to forgive myself and others. To love unconditionally. I learned to speak my truth with love. I learned to be grateful for Life—the greatest teacher—for constantly bringing me back to myself, back into my heart where only Love resides. No matter what is going on in my life, I love. I AM LOVE and so ARE YOU.

I love my life and everything in it exactly the way it is. I love and accept every given moment as I take another breath knowing my true wisdom means: I am Love and I have The Free Will to create The Life I choose.

Part Two

I Choose to Write

In the second part of this book I would like to share with you, Dear Reader, pages from my journal, experiences from the last three years of my life when I again found my passion for writing, which made me think about my school days when I enjoyed writing essays.

I never imagined I could write a book. When I paged through a magazine on the flight to Canada, I had wondered if I would ever be able to read and write in English. Now, writing this book in English seems natural to me. I always loved reading and studying on my own. I am a student of life. Curious, I believe every moment is an opportunity for me to explore, to grow, and to expand. I see every moment as a gift to experience something new in life.

I came here to learn and to teach. I believe every human life is a book of unique teachings and the wisdom we earn through life and share with others is how we can learn from each other. I am thankful for this truth I have found. I call it—My Truth. I now know that coming here, to this part of the world, was something I needed to do to complete my Soul mission.

I was never homesick. I always felt at home here in Canada. I love visiting my homeland Slovakia, but I love coming home to Canada. I feel my home is where my heart is.

Friday, June 17, 2011 - 6:00 pm

Seeing My Mother Proud

It is a beautiful sunny summer day. I am sitting here at the park by the water. My birthday was few days ago, and I am thinking of my mother who passed away years ago. I notice a seagull close to me and feel it is a messenger. For a moment I close my eyes, feeling the warm gentle breeze on my face and reflect on the greatness of my life.

My memories take me back to five years ago when I decided to take a yoga teacher training course. At the beginning of the course, during a guided meditation, I saw myself sitting in a room of my house. Not a house I recognized from this lifetime. There was a wooden table and a chair in the middle of the room. The house was older and cozy, with small windows and a wooden floor. Everything looked perfectly clean and organized. I saw myself sitting at the wooden table, writing a book. I was alone, wearing a creamy dress with pink squares. I felt inspired as I wrote my book with feelings of enthusiasm and love. As I wrote, I had a vision of my mother watching me from the window. She smiled, seeming proud, and I felt her happiness within me. The feeling from this meditation reminded me of the time during this life time when she told me of her happiness at my birth. In the vision, she continued observing me quietly, without words, with unconditional love. Her face said she gave me everything she could, her best self, her loving self. The vision in my meditation seemed to be from the seventeenth century and my mother in this lifetime had been my mother then. This meditation was a profound experience.

Thank you, Mama. No matter what happened while we shared our lives as you walked this physical world, your love is a memory I cherish forever in my heart. I am a blessed daughter and I feel your loving presence everywhere. I am also a proud mother, and I know what a great feeling it is to love a daughter. I searched the significance of the seagull and found: it might be a sign to break out of your routine, show the world your potential. The seagull represents freedom, adaptation, communication, and resourcefulness.

Wisdom

- *Be proud of who you are and thankful for your parents and children.*

Saturday, July 2, 2011, 7:40 am, Oakville

Mother

It is a beautiful summer morning, sunny and warm. I got up and meditated. As I observed my breath and thoughts, I heard the birds outside. After a while, I heard my inner voice whispering to me, "Mother. Write about mother."

I never know what I will write about, I never think about it. I observe my breath and listen to the whisper of my Soul—my guidance. Today I will write about my mother, every mother, and Mother Earth. I believe there is a reason behind this message, as there is behind everything that happens in our life.

When I hear the word mother I see and feel women that represent nurturing, love, peace, an open heart, beauty, wisdom, courage, intuition, strength and creativity. My mother was all that. I did not realize this while I was growing up, that came much later. She went through many challenges, her life was not always easy, but she remained strong.

I see her deep dark, big eyes, and dark hair in my mind's eye now. She left this physical plane seventeen years ago. I feel her love in my heart. I know she loved me even though she did not express as much affection as I wanted to experience while growing up. Now, I see it through different eyes. She had a lot to handle in her short life. As I think of her, great memories come to my mind. I remember the good, nurturing food she prepared for the family. She took great care of our home, garden, and animals. I remember her creativity. She knitted sweaters for me and I still remember my favourite one; it was white in colour. She helped build our new house. She cared for her parents when they were elderly, all the while working part time and raising a family. I really admire my mother for who she was, a wise woman always wanting the best for everyone. This whole week I felt her presence. Yesterday I went for a walk, and I saw my friend, Mary. A few days prior, I met a woman whose name was also Mary. I could feel these synchronicities had meaning. My mother's name was Maria, the Slovak version of Mary. In the afternoon, my husband and I went for a drive and we saw two statues of the Virgin Mary in two different gardens. I had never seen a Virgin Mary statue in a garden before. I knew the presence of my mother's energy was telling me something.

The next morning I went to an Angel Workshop. I feel I am strongly connected to the angelic realm. The woman who organized the workshop did a short angel card reading for all of us. I picked a card and she asked me: "Did your mom cross over?" I said yes and she replied, "Your mom wants to tell you that she is very proud of you."

I could feel her presence. It was not the first time I felt her presence since she had passed.

I am fortunate to be a daughter to my special mother. Love and understanding connects us. I know how important and how precious the feeling of the unconditional love connection is, being a mother myself and having a special daughter.

It does not matter if we are in our physical body or not, love always exists. Love is forever. Love is the Light we are made of, which enters and leaves the physical body. It is an energy that never dies. Without love we would not be here. Love is the foundation of every human being.

Love is what you can build on, especially the love between a mother and her child. It is strong, pure, unconditional and forever.

Thank you, Mama, for being the Light on my path. Blessings to all Mothers.

Wisdom

- *In your mother's womb your body grew. Cherish your mother.*

- *We all have different mothers, but we also share one—our Mother Earth.*

- *I give thanks to Mother Earth for all the gifts in my life.*

Sunday, July 3, 2011 - 3:21 pm

Automatic Writing

Our mind categorizes days into good and bad. It is human nature to like some experiences better than others. The deep truth is: all experiences are valuable for our Soul's growth. When I reached the point in my life when I stopped categorizing with the labels of good and bad, my life became easier. When I label something as bad it feels bad, but when I instead attach the words it is, it becomes neutral and easier to handle.

What I find that really works for me is automatic writing. I take my notebook everywhere with me. You may choose to talk to friends, family, or people you think can help you find a solution, but ultimately your heart knows the best solution. All these people may help you to some extent, but all their solutions will come from their point of view, which can be fundamentally different from yours. In the end, everyone else's solutions may be confusing and make the situation look more complicated than it is.

We all go through times when we search for answers and writing is one way to find them. It will likely take practice. The more I did it, the deeper the answers became, as well as the feelings of peace that followed. When I participate in automatic writing, I know I am not alone and I am supported and not judged or given advice that does not resonate with me. Everything I hear is from my Higher Self and it makes sense, and I feel stronger and uplifted rather than victimized by the situation.

Today I used automatic writing to find an answer. I did not focus on the situation I needed help with. I simply sat, took a few deep breaths, reminded myself to relax, and then I asked the Spirit a question, "What is most important for me to know right now?" I could feel that changes in my work life were coming: perhaps something different than hairdressing. Then I listened to my heart and waited until my hand started writing.

This is what came through...

"Your life is precious. Whatever you are facing now will pass. It is happening for your better future. You know you need to be strong; things are shifting. Be yourself and sail on the waters of life as they are presented to you now. Everything is okay as it is. You just needed to come to a quiet place to realize that. You need this down time: the experience you are going through has value. Maybe you do not realize that now, but things are changing, and you will find out the reason why later. Stay in your heart love is always there. Focus on your creativity and potential. Choose freedom. Do not look around, just sail your way. Stay in the present moment. Life is beautiful and full of surprises. Be the best you can be, stay connected to the love, peace, and harmony in your heart. You are strong, loving, and always a bright Light. Do not worry about anything. Enjoy every moment of your life. Enjoy the NOW. Go and take a bath and read. Love is within you."

My hand stopped writing and I felt at home again in my heart. Strong feelings of trust and knowing that what the Source wrote through my hand, was my truth. I went home, took a salt bath, read a few pages of a book, and was grounded and ready to continue my day in loving vibrations. Most of our situations are not as bad as we see them. Sometimes we just need to spend time in solitude and focus on the love and light within us. Sometimes our answer comes in a neutral form and it means that is all we need to know at that time; more will be revealed to us when the time comes. Trust is essential.

Wisdom

- *Know all is well in your life.*

- *Know life is an education, and during lifetimes we learn how to love ourselves and others unconditionally.*

- *Forgive yourself, and others, and move on.*
- *True freedom comes from knowing your Light in your heart.*

- *Bless situations and everyone who is teaching you lessons.*

Saturday, December 31, 2011 - 9:36 pm

Last Day of the Year

2011 is ending and I want to thank you, Daniela, my daughter, for this beautiful writing journal you gave me for Christmas. I know you have believed in my dream that I can write a book and now you are telling me, with this gift, that it is coming true.

I dedicate this book to you. I want to leave this book as a legacy, a piece in our lineage. Our descendants may one day want to know who we were and it is my privilege to leave this book for our children, and for humanity. I was the first in our family to come to Canada to start this journey and I consider this book a jewel, a written history about who we were, where we began, for your children and theirs, for generations to come.

There is much to know about life itself, about our lives, families, experiences, and the love we share. Life is challenging and beautiful. Love and faith helped me through all my challenges.

I know, Daniela, that you know this Truth. You live your life from your heart. You share your light and love with me, and everyone who crosses your path. May you always shine with your Light. I thank you from my heart that you chose me to be your Mama.

Love always.

Monday, January 2, 2012 - 8:50 pm

Beginning of Something New

It is the New Year. I am thankful for my life. I trust every new moment that is born. I see every moment as beautiful, with deep meaning. In this moment, I feel deep gratitude for who I have become. I am reflecting on my life.

Writing a book has been my silent dream for more than half of my life, and now it is becoming a reality. I trust that it will be published. I believe it was written on my path, by me, and that is why it has been my strong desire. My Soul remembers.

Sometimes, time elapses before our desire becomes reality. We must be patient and trusting. I needed that time to go through my life experiences otherwise this book would not have come to be.

Everything has a time and purpose. I learned to allow things to happen instead of making things happen. It is the art of living wisely, to be able to allow. Miracles happen when we allow. Life becomes a miracle when we allow and trust.

Wisdom

- *Miracles are everywhere, be willing to see them.*

- *Life is a miracle. You are the miracle.*

- *Love the miracle you see in the mirror.*

- *Allow miracles to come your way. Accept miracles.*

Sunday, February 26, 2012 – 6:00 am

Love is All That Matters

On this beautiful day Daniela and her boyfriend, Jean-Philippe (we call him JP), came over for lunch to celebrate her birthday. The greatest gift of all is when we spend time together. Memories of sharing time, as a family, can't be taken from us. They are always within us and for us. They are priceless gifts. Remembering and cherishing times of love is remembering who we are. Life is precious with all these simple loving moments we share in the circle of our own families. There is nothing more memorable than time spent with family and friends, where we share our hearts.

Love is all that matters.

Love in Heart

The heart is the place where we keep our precious moments.
The heart is our treasure box, which can never be misplaced.
We can always create more treasured moments.
Life is the opportunity to collect our earthly treasures.
We can always expand the experience of love in our heart.
There is no limit for love.
Love is unconditional, timeless, space-less and infinite
We can count on love.
It always supports us.
Love creates everything that is meaningful and beautiful.
Love is something we can't lose or find.
Love is always there, even if we forget.
Love never forgets us.
It is like a sky.
It is always there.
It is only when we forget to look up we don't see the beauty of the sky.
Always look up and feel the love of your heart.

Happy Birthday, Daniela.

Blessings and love to you always, my daughter. I wish for you to celebrate your loving heart on this day and for many years to come.

I love you.

Sunday, March 4, 2012 - 2:30 pm

Blessings To All Women on Planet Earth

While enjoying a sunny Sunday afternoon, I closed my eyes, loving the feeling of the hot sun on my face.

In my daydream, I had a vision, I did not recognize the place but I did recognize the people. I saw myself on the beach on a warm, sunny day. Beautiful young horses approached me, running on the edge of the calm, shining water. They were happy to see me waiting for them on the beach. Finally, they came to me and I felt a greatness just being with them. It was an amazing union. I felt only love when I touched them. Their hide was like velvet, soft and pure. It was a beautiful experience. As we played, I turned around and saw a beach house with a big verandah in front. My husband was standing there and I felt his happiness to see me playing with our young horses.

This moment was filled with everything: love, sunshine, water, and people I know. Even though I saw only my husband, I know there were many people around me from the unseen world. Then I saw them too, as though they were made of glass. They were coming out of the water towards me. They all looked happy and loving, coming to me, making a circle and we were celebrating each other's presence. It felt peaceful and genuine. We all knew each other, and we were dancing.

Then I saw my daughter, my mother, and my husband's daughters. I saw my grandmothers and my sister. All the women in my family, women I've worked with and many others I know. It was truly amazing. This union felt strong. We all celebrated our lives. We all knew we have only love to share. We were together before, and we met again in this life.

I am sending love and light, to all these women—divine sisters—only blessings from my heart. May every woman on our Earth be blessed and find the truth.

Symbolic meaning of horses: Power, Grace, Beauty, Nobility, Strength, and Freedom

These words perfectly describe women. As I observed these words and their meaning a poem came to my awareness.

Message to all women from the horse:

>Power of Your Love
>Grace of Your Word
>Beauty of Your Smile
>Nobility of Your Heart
>Strength of Your Wisdom
>Brings Freedom to the World

Saturday, March 24, 2012 - 8:30 am

Be Who You Were Born To Be

When you forget who you are you believe others' views of who you are. When you remember your heart's truth you are strong, you take action, and you create a fulfilling life. You believe in yourself and you know you are whole and complete.

Your life is not about what you do. It is about who you are. Because everything you do, shows who you are. What you do comes from the state of your consciousness. Our consciousness is always evolving.

Wisdom

- *Love to create your life. Accept, learn, forgive, let go, and love.*

- *Shine your Light and move through your life with courage and grace.*

- *Never give up and be who you were born to be. It always feels right.*

- *May you always feel the love of your heart.*

Tuesday, April 3, 2012 - 8:32 am

New Morning

This morning I woke up and listened to the beautiful birds singing outside. I walked outside in my garden and I saw a blue jay, a cardinal, and sparrows. Nature is stunning. Nothing is comparable to the awakening of the new day.

The sun rising brings us a new day with opportunities to learn, expand, and love. We rise to a new life, new dreams, and new life expansion. We have another opportunity to be our best selves. I'm grateful to see the sun coming up again. Every day is a gift.

Wisdom

- We are love connected as One.

- We are like flowers reaching for sunlight.

- Divine Light shines through our hearts.

Friday, April 20, 2012 - 1:40 pm

Spirituality

In my eyes, spirituality is the ability to live from the heart in the present moment. This creates the best outcome for each of us and for all.

To me, spirituality means to be connected with the essence of who we are—our own truth. I believe there is nothing more beautiful and fulfilling in our lives than knowing who we are on a deeper energy level; knowing our Soul. Beauty comes when we are able to be true to ourselves and love ourselves unconditionally, without judgment.

In this physical world we have an opportunity to experience duality. Without experiencing duality we are unable to know what we prefer. With free will we have a choice to choose what we prefer. I believe the purpose of our life is peace and joy, and when we live in a state of peace and joy, we create the most beautiful and precious experiences for ourselves and others. It is not only our purpose, but our responsibility to live our lives with awareness of a connection to the Source so that we can live with meaning. We are here to know and to use our full potential.

Spirituality, in my eyes, is also the ability to feel a connection with nature and all lives. When we live our truth, we hold high vibrations in our energy field and we know we are complete—whole. With this awareness life becomes blissful, not an obstacle. We attract people and situations with the same vibrations as our own. We start to see the same world with different eyes, and we realize that there are two physical worlds coexisting on our planet Earth. It is a constructive and destructive world.

I feel there is no need to go into detail of the world of destruction. Likely, we all have experienced that world in the past, but when we live our Soul truth we focus on and experience the world of bliss, by choice. Even through difficulties we are able to see the beauty of nature, we experience love and the goodness of people's hearts. We feel bliss when smelling flowers, we gift ourselves with time to relax and enjoy life every day. We do not rush anywhere anymore because what we need comes to us. It is magical to live that truth. We accept the weather when it is sunny and warm, and we accept it when it is cloudy and raining, because we understand the law of nature, the world of duality. We know the rain is a blessing; it is food for trees, flowers and for us. We accept the present moment as it is. We are not judging people and situations, we allow, we observe, learn and grow. We understand challenges in our lives because we know that they are a gift from the Divine. The challenges are for us to learn and to grow. When we overcome a challenge with love, we feel stronger and wiser than before; we shine like a diamond! The more pressure we experience in nature, the more brilliant the diamond becomes. Once we go through a challenge, we can shine our true light much brighter and then we can share our inner beauty and the wisdom we have gained with others.

Humans are social beings; we like to be connected and connection on the heart level is much needed. With that deep connection, life feels rich; we share our essence, which is unconditional love. Through the heart connection we feel oneness and strength. We feel we are strongly supported by Mother Earth.

It is the blissful experience of life, like watching a child playing, walking with the one you love, or smelling a flower, priceless moments of living life. It is also the acceptance of everything and everyone without judgment.

Wisdom

- *Enjoy the simplicity of life.*

- *Live in harmony with yourself and others.*

- *Live your life as an example for others.*

- *Live the wisdom of your heart and share it with others.*

- *Live in deep understanding of our Universe and Creator.*

Sunday, May 13, 2012 - 10:08 am

Thank You for My Life

We are experiencing a unique time on the planet; the shift of consciousness. We all go through changes, small and big. We are becoming more connected with our true self; our Soul. If you are reading this book, you probably question who we are, where we come from, and what our purpose is on this planet Earth. When we understand life from our soul's perspective we allow life to unfold, and we see our life as the greatest gift from the Creator. We are here to experience the beauty and richness of life, oneness through our hearts.

Today is Mother's Day. I am thankful for the experience of being a mother. God blessed me with the gift of my daughter. Bringing a child into the world is an experience that a mother never forgets.

Experiencing that circle of life is profound. There are different occasions we celebrate, such as mother's day, father's day, birthdays, and other holidays, but the greatest celebration is the celebration of life. It opens us up to gratitude for every breath and every step we take. We experience the beauty of who we are and the beauty and power of nature. We feel vibrant and we feel connected to our Creator. We are able to be more present, to be aware birds flying and tree branches moving, listening to the waves in the lake, watching children playing and laughing...

It is time to celebrate now. You do not need to wait for a special day or event to come. Now is special. It is your life and it is you who is special. It is never too late to see who you are, to love all that you are, and to rejoice who you are.

I am thankful to my mother for my life. Thank you, Creator, for the gift of being a mother. Thank you to Mother Earth for all your earthly gifts and blessings.

Wisdom

- *Celebrate your life, and the life of others.*

- *Celebrate the life of your child.*

- *Celebrate the life of the baby you may be expecting and feel the greatness of the gift within your body.*

- *Experience the depth of your life through breath.*

- *Live with gratitude for every breath you take.*

- *Within your breath, feel your inner child.*

Tuesday, May 22, 2012 - 12:40 pm

In My Garden, Inspired by Nature

I am always amazed when I observe nature. It is magnificent. I see nature as an abundance of unconditional love. Nature inspires me. It is peaceful and harmonious.

As I am observing my garden and embracing this present moment, my golden retriever, Lopci, came to me and then turned away and lied down behind me. He is very sensitive. He knows this is the time for me to write the next chapter in this book, and he lets me do that. Usually when he comes to me, he wants to play, but because he senses I am writing, he lets me be. Animals do not speak, but they do understand. They have their own language. Animals communicate on a deeper level, the energy level that is our essence. They are sensitive to the energies of people and everything around them.

To be in harmony with nature we need to spend time with nature every day, to observe and to feel the connection with nature, birds and animals. When we do so, we become more in harmony with the nature of who we are. A great way to connect deeply is through meditation. When I meditate, I sit quietly and observe with my inner eye. I know everything I need to know in life, for my well-being, for my fulfillment, will be revealed to me in the perfect divine time.

Our truth lies in the simplicity of our life. Observing nature, listening to the birds, observing the dog or simply being still with my eyes closed, take me into the present moment. The present moment is where the power of true knowingness lies. It is all we have and all that is important. It holds all our answers.

Wisdom

- *In the present moment we have access to the deep wisdom of who we are.*

- *We are blessed with unique gifts, sharing them is essential for the balance of humanity.*

- *When we know and share our gifts we feel complete.*

- *Self-realization and living from the place of truth, from your heart, will set you free.*

- *Never underestimate your own greatness.*

- *Trust yourself and this present moment.*

- *Know who you are, your essence.*

- *Be conscious of your thoughts, they create your today and your future.*

- *The present moment is a powerful place from which we create.*

- *Observing nature is one of the greatest tools to bring us back into the now.*

- *When we love nature, we love ourselves, as we are part of nature.*

- *Self-realization comes from within, in the present moment.*

- *We are pure Divine Love.*

Wednesday, May 30, 2012 - 10:49 pm

Messages

Today I attended a seminar about spirituality in health care. When I came home I picked up an angel card with a message. The card is the Footprint card and its message is:

"You have beautiful intentions of doing well in this world and having a lasting and positive effect on the planet. This was a part of the divine plan you created for yourself before you came here. Those inner aspirations you feel and the daydreams associated with them are the whisperings of your Soul calling you to your purpose. This is all part of your journey. The time has come to take the steps necessary to set this dream in motion." Destiny Cards by Cheryl Lee Harnish.

I believe the Spirit, the Creator, the One, whatever we wish to call IT talks to us all the time. IT guides us and gives us messages. I like the playfulness of the Spirit. I trust and I always ask for messages from the Spirit. IT gives me messages in many different ways, through books, songs, through people, numbers, symbols, and animals. Sometimes I get messages through feelings. I simply know. Sometimes an idea comes and I feel it is right for me. The destiny card I picked tonight confirmed what I've been hearing from the subtle voice of my Soul when I meditate.

I believe in the goodness of people and the world. When I close my eyes, in my mind's eye I can see that it is possible for us to create a world of peace and joy. I intend to participate with love in this process of growth and expansion. The world can only transform when each of us transforms, when we change our limited beliefs.

Thursday, May 31, 2012 – 2:12 pm

Divine speaks through Synchronicities—Number 747

For the last few months, I have been seeing the number 747 everywhere. Today it was more obvious than ever. As I drove to Toronto around 6 pm, my inner voice whispered, "You will see 747" so I started paying attention to license plates and soon, I passed a car with the number 747. I also noticed the first two letters were my initials—DS.

On my way home hours later, I was on the highway and heard the whisper again. I started paying attention to license plates, and a few minutes later a car with the number 747 passed me. What really opened my eyes was that it was the same car I had seen earlier, with the initials—DS on the license plate. In that moment I felt shivers all over my body. I felt the presence of the Divine very strongly. I wondered what the meaning was behind this number as I believe there is meaning behind every synchronicity.

Doreen Virtue's Angel Book states that 747 means, "The Angels are telling you to soar high in the direction of your dreams."

We all have dreams and visions in our lives. Our dreams are in our consciousness for a reason. It is our Soul speaking to us because we have a destiny to complete. I believe we planned our life before we came into the physical world. We chose what we want to experience.

Do you see repeating numbers? Pay attention, there is meaning behind them. My dream is to see this book serve those who are seeking to live their heart's purpose. What is your dream, Dear Reader?

Friday, June 1, 2012 - 8:30 am

This Book Will Reach Many

I enjoy the process of my life and I trust and believe that everything is unfolding in my best interest. There are many synchronicities around me. Life is meaningful when we pay attention to these synchronicities. Yesterday, I visited a lady who does intuitive guidance through numerology. I am always curious to try new things and I am open-minded. I pay attention to messages intended especially for me. I asked her if she sees anything that would be helpful for me to know, because I feel changes are coming my way. She replied: "Do you write? I feel what you write will reach millions." Hmm, I did not expect her to say that.

I feel deep within me the message in this book is important. This book wants to be born. I feel it is part of my life's purpose. In this book, I am sharing my life's experience. My intention is to complete and leave this book as a gift to my family as well as a gift to humanity. It would be a great reward to know that this book reached millions, to know, it reminded others how to understand their own life and Light within. I believe we all are born with gifts to share with our fellow humans. Perhaps thousands or millions are ready to receive our gifts. I believe our gifts are equally important. It is essential to trust and enjoy the process without attachment to the outcome.

What this woman said was good to hear, but I am not attached to it. I love writing this book. Just for me, for fun, for the feeling that I'm doing what I enjoy. When I write, I feel I am a channel through which the Divine can speak. We are all channels of Divine Light. I encourage you to stay connected to your heart and channel your gifts. It is rewarding.

Sunday, June 3, 2012 – 11:15 am

In My Dream

Last night I had a dream about a girl who wanted to come to this world to experience its duality. In her life, she helped many people around her. It was her mission and she did it with love and joy. In many different lifetimes before, she experienced torture and punishment for being a healer; a wise one.

To her good fortune, she had many teachers around her. She loved unconditionally. Her presence was a healing one. Many people appreciated her, but some took advantage of her. The experience of duality made her stronger. All those experiences gave her opportunities to choose from. In one of her lives, she was a teacher and people called her Red Hair. Besides teaching the usual subjects taught in school, she taught children how to love themselves. She knew that self-love was important.

When I awoke I reflected on my dream. The importance of self-love deeply resonates with me. It is only when we truly love ourselves, without judgment, that we can love others.

When we learn how to love ourselves when we are children we will love ourselves when we reach adulthood. When we love ourselves, we act from our heart—from love vibration. Out of this state we are able to love others and everything around us unconditionally. We understand the value of all our experiences, and feel no need to harm the Self, other people or nature. When we focus on deep self-love, we create harmony. It is a gift we can teach our children by example. First of all, we must let go of everything that keeps us from self-love, especially false beliefs, guilt, regrets, criticism and all low vibration emotions.

It is time to embrace our hearts and to teach love with our presence. When we choose to live from the heart we become the teachings—teachings of love.

Wisdom

- *The best teacher is the one who teaches by example.*

- *The most important thing in life is to love ourselves unconditionally.*

- *In this amazing universal evolution, life is more meaningful every day.*

- *We don't know what our heart has in store for us until we go within.*

- *In every moment of life, each of us is the student and the teacher.*

- *Learn and teach with a loving heart.*

Saturday, June 9, 2012 - 8:02 am

Listening to the Inner Voice

I learned to pay attention to my inner voice. We are all born to this world with our own inner voice, our sixth sense; intuition. It is the life within us, the guidance. We are more attuned to it at an early age. Children are intuitive. We can never lose intuition, but in this busy world we may forget to pay attention or even resist listening. Though we may not be listening, it remains dormant—waiting to be heard.

We always have that subtle voice speaking to us. It is up to us to listen or not. The best way to hear our intuition is to sit in silence, practice deep relaxation where we can quiet our mind. People call this meditation, but I often call it my time. Sometimes practicing a few minutes of meditation is all we need. I like to do it in nature, while I take a bath, or just sitting quietly in a comfortable chair. It is how I like to connect with my essence, my truth. It is how I get messages from my higher self.

Many times when I have sat in silence my inner voice has said: "One day you will write a book about your life experiences." This sounded great, but I was not sure if I believed it. My mind said "maybe not" or "it's just your imagination—it won't happen." At that time, I was not aware of the difference between a Soul voice and mind talk. Now I know our Soul speaks to us all the time. Guiding us with new ideas. It wants us to complete our destiny. When we pay attention to that subtle voice instead of pushing it away, it is easier for us to go through life. When I pay attention and I ask for guidance I get more information, and I create without effort.

Synchronicities

Yesterday morning I went to a seminar about energy healing. Before I left, my inner voice told me to turn on the radio and to pay attention to what I hear first, so I did. I really like how playful the Divine is. When I turned it on, a song was ending. Immediately after, the announcer said that someone's book was coming out that day, and I felt shivers all over my body. When I arrived at the seminar, the speaker began by saying: "pay attention to synchronicities," and I shivered again.

After the seminar, I went on with my day. I had lunch, went to work, and had a relaxing bath in the evening. After bathing, I took my angel cards and I asked for a message before going to bed. I love my angel cards. They are always accurate! The card I picked said: "Write a journal; it is important to write about your life; there is an important message."

So, I am writing with love in my heart and I believe that one day this journal of mine will bring a message to many people, like you, Dear Reader, because you are ready to hear it.

With love and gratitude to my Higher Self and my guidance.

Sunday, June 10, 2012 - 8:01 am

Message in the Feather

After yesterday's yoga class, I told the participants to watch for a feather today. I do not know why I said it, I just did. We hadn't been talking about animals or feathers. After they left, my inner voice whispered: "You too, watch for the feather, there will be a message for you." It was a very clear voice. I thought nothing of it, I just enjoyed the fun feeling behind the soft voice, and my day began to unfold and I forgot all about the feather.

It was a hot day and I had things to do. I wanted to prepare a pasta salad for a potluck for the drum circle my husband and I planned to attend that evening. I also had a client scheduled later on. I went outside to give my dog, Lopci, cold water and I saw that he was hot. He was looking at me with his shiny eyes and I could read his face "I'd like to go to the lake and cool down in the water." My mind was resistant thinking I was too busy. My dog kept looking at me with his big happy eyes and I got an image of him playing in the water. My urge to take him to the lake was strong, so I pushed away the thoughts that I don't have time and listened to the voice of my Soul.

I couldn't resist the power within me, moving my body, getting in to the car. I didn't want to resist it because I have learned that when I do resist the guidance, I feel it is not right or I struggle with whatever I choose to do instead. So, we jumped in the car, both now happy. I knew if I took half an hour off and went to the park, I would still have time to manage what I planned to do. After all, I realized when I go with the flow of life everything comes easier anyway.

At the park, I let Lopci out and in less than a minute he was cooling in the crystal clear water. My heart sang. I watched him as he chased after a big stick I had thrown into the water. I was totally in the present moment, connected with Mother Earth and nature. Nothing else was important;

nothing was missing from that moment. It was filled with all—with love, with the fullness and richness of life. I caught myself smiling, playing with my dog and feeling as though I had plenty of time. I felt happy, childlike and free. I felt the oneness with everything around me. I saw people walking, children playing, an older couple sitting on a bench laughing and hugging each other. I saw the sweetness of life that I miss seeing when I am in a hurry and thinking that something else is more important than following my guidance, the inner voice which speaks to us all.

I had a great twenty minutes playing with my dog and observing life. As I was walking back to the car, I almost stepped on two feathers lying on the ground. I heard the voice remind me to watch for the feather. I smiled. I picked them up, looking at them, asking myself, "What is the message?" As I thought this, two girls, perhaps six and eight years old, approached me, their father following them. They said they liked my dog and happily started to pet him. The younger girl noticed my feathers and she asked me what I was going to do with them. Her question surprised me and I told her I might put them somewhere in my back yard. She looked at me with her big blue eyes full of excitement and said, "Maybe you should put ink in them and write."

I had shivers all over my body; her sweet voice had left me speechless. She then picked up a small feather from the grass, handed it to me and wished me good luck. I held my two big writing feathers and the small feather for good luck. I was stunned. I knew Divine was speaking to me through this beautiful little girl. Before they left, her sister added, "You can make a dream catcher." The moment was priceless. Before they ran off, I thanked them. I had no other words.

It was a priceless moment. I stopped. I wanted to feel my body, my heart...my feelings. I felt the energy around my body expand. I felt connectedness with the Higher Power in charge of this experience. I felt it was a strong message. A message to write, the purpose of my life, the feeling of wholeness, the uniqueness of the gifts I was born with, and knowing that my gifts need to be shared.

I then realized why I had verbalized the feather message to my students—it had been meant for me. A message I would have missed if I had listened to my mind rather than my heart—taking my loving dog to the park. Seeing the Divine through his shiny eyes made me go, and I am thankful I listened to the Divine.

The message came to me through these little girls whom I may never see again. They were there to vocalize what I had been hearing in silence: write a book, pay attention to your dreams, there are messages for you.

With love and much gratitude to the Divine, and to those two precious angels in the bodies of girls I met in Coronation Park.

Wisdom

- *Life is amazing when we do not resist it and allow it to unfold.*

- *Allow your life to unfold and enjoy the jewels that come out of it.*

- *The voice of Higher Self always guides us with love.*

- *Sharing your gifts with the world is sharing your essence with the world.*

Monday, June 11, 2012 – 6:16 am

World of Duality

We live in a world of duality. There is the world of love that creates beauty, peace, well-being, and there is the world of fear that creates chaos. We have free will and the power to choose which world we want to experience. If we choose to focus on absolute love and the beauty of life around us, that is what we will experience and we will create more of it. If we choose to focus on the chaos around us, that is what we will experience and create more of.

The choice is yours. It is important to ask the question, "What do I choose?" and to be aware of our thoughts. Our thoughts create our reality now and our reality in the future.

Wisdom

- *Choose wisely—the moment never returns again for you to make a different choice.*

- *Choose love, beauty, peace, nature and your life will be more of what you want, it can't be otherwise. We always experience the law of attraction: what we focus on, we experience.*

- *Know that what you choose for yourself, you choose for all. We are connected through our heart vibrations.*

- *Choose to make a difference for yourself and for all, differences that are worth living.*

Tuesday, June 12, 2012 - 8:07 am

Relationship

The greatest, and most beautiful, relationship we can create is the relationship with the Self. Love is divine and unlimited. It has no boundaries. We can choose to love ourselves unconditionally or not. Whichever choice we make, the Universe always supports us.

With every breath we take, there are infinite options and opportunities on how to live, and what steps to take next. When our actions feel right, it means we love our Self. The better we feel inside, the more in harmony we are with our heart.

When we do things that benefit our health and well-being we feel at peace, at ease, and worthy. The unconditional love vibration is the highest one, it is the essence we are made of, and when our body and aura hold high vibrations, we feel good.

When we live authentically with a feeling of love and gratitude, only then can we create loving and lasting relationships with other people who vibrate on the same level. It is the universal law of attraction which is in action all the time, whether we are aware of it or not. Love will always attract love. What we offer to the world will always come back to us.

Sometimes in life we forget to love ourselves unconditionally and we attract experiences in life that we are not happy with. We are fortunate, because we can choose to remember love again. Every day is a new beginning and a new opportunity to choose to feel good, to choose to overcome challenges, and to learn from experience. The key to a good relationship is forgiveness, to forgive yourself and others.

To create a good relationship with the Self, do something you like. I like to go for walks, dance, watch the stars at night, read a book, or take a bath... Do anything that will make your heart dance, or do nothing and just be. It is good to do something for ourselves every day, as a reminder to be our true Self, to remember playfulness, to do something that makes us remember our divinity. As we change the way we treat ourselves, we begin to experience the changes in the outside world because everything is a reflection of how we feel about ourselves. People and situations reflect back to us our state of being. When we give ourselves more care, more time, and quality experiences, we become more energetically aware. When we are appreciative towards life, the world will reflect the same back to us.

When we become aware of our connection to divinity, we are stronger and more creative. Everything we need for life comes our way effortlessly. Life and every relationship become meaningful.

Wisdom

- *We can create a deeper relationship with Self through meditation, stillness, focusing on heart and breath. Our breath is a signature of the Soul.*

- *All relationships are a reflection of the relationship we have with Self.*

- *Nobody and nothing can make us feel good or bad—we choose how we feel.*

- *If we think somebody can make us feel bad, we give our power away.*

- *When we have a loving relationship with our Self we choose not to give our power away.*

Wednesday, June 13, 2012 - 7:15 am

Sounds of a Summer Morning

It is a beautiful Wednesday morning. I am sitting in my garden, a place I love to be. I watch plants I planted over the years, growing, and some blooming. I feel the richness of this present moment as I observe my life unfolding.

I observe the beauty of nature, my great teacher. When I close my eyes I hear the sound of life. I find the sound of the morning peaceful and fresh. I see every morning as a new opportunity for new experiences, new lessons, and new treasures to come. I can hear birds singing. I can hear the morning breeze moving through the trees. Nature sounds different each moment and it creates harmony and beauty. It is soothing to my body, mind and soul.

I close my eyes again and I feel great love and appreciation for this moment. I am grateful for my life and the experience of this morning's nature song.

Thursday, June 14, 2012 - 7:15 am

Great Day at the Spa

We just came home from a Spa in Collingwood, Ontario. My husband and I love to go there to nurture our Souls. It is a beautiful place in natural surroundings. People enjoy themselves in silence. After a day spent there, I feel relaxed and rejuvenated. I sat down and I picked an Angel card, asking what the message is for my birthday. The card I picked said:

Birth of Angels:"You are surrounded with the support of the angelic realm. You play an important role on earth in uplifting the planet. The angels are here to help you in every way they can. Remember, you are not alone on this journey. Your gifts are special and needed. These divine beings are here with you to aid you in becoming fully who you are truly meant to be. Now you will see your path opening more than ever before." www.FractalArt.ca

I enjoyed my birthday gift. A peaceful time spent with my loving husband under the sun, in nature. I loved the message from the angels at the end of the day. It is what I feel deep inside my heart, that I am surrounded with angels and guided to share the gifts I was born with. It is my greatest wish for my birthday to be authentic and to be in service to All. I am ready to walk on the path that is unfolding before me, fully embracing my true Self.

With love and gratitude to my loving Family and Angels.

Friday, June 15, 2012 - 10:00 am

Wisdom

- *When we have the courage to try something new in our life, chances are we will likely experience the life we seek.*

- *Trying new things may be a challenge, but worthwhile. We do not know what we miss if we do not try.*

- *There is always creative energy flowing through us wanting to be expressed. Express that energy for your benefit and enjoyment. When you do, you do it for the benefit and enjoyment of humanity.*

- *With evolution always comes the new, let the new unfold in you and observe what happens, you will be delightfully surprised.*

- *It is not only your birthday that is a special day. It is your life and YOU that is special; celebrate and give gratitude for your life every day.*

Saturday, June 16, 2012 - 7:30 am

New in Life

It is time for me to write again. I hear I should write about new experiences in life. Sometimes people ask me how many hours I write each day. I never plan what I will write or when. There are parts of my writing that do not come from my mind, because I write without thinking. I quiet my mind and simply write what I hear, as though it is flowing through me. I do not try to make it happen. I let it happen spontaneously without any effort. I tried a few times to sit down and write because I had time, but nothing came...

Up to my early forties, I lived what I could call a normal life. I had a loving family, friends, a full-time job, a house, car, and vacations. We would occasionally go to the movies, go to parties, and visit friends. I held on to certain beliefs and patterns I had picked up throughout my life. I knew it was all part of my journey and it was okay. However, there were times I felt there must be more to life, something I could not name or buy. Many times I felt I was in a box and I had the urge to discover a new way of living within me.

I questioned why I felt like something was missing in my life. Why I felt there was something hidden in my life that wanted to be discovered. I looked around and saw I had everything I needed and wanted. My loved ones and I were healthy. We lived in a home we owned, in a nice neighborhood. I had a job I liked. "What more is there for me," I kept asking myself. The more I asked, the clearer the answer became. What I sought was not physical. I had a feeling it was within me. I realized that the feeling was within me for as long as I could remember, but I was too busy with my physical life to pay attention to it, to embrace it, and most of all, to live IT.

I remembered the feeling of freedom, curiosity and creativity when I was a little girl living in a small village. I remembered the freedom, the fearlessness, and the adventures I had lived. I felt deep within that still existed and that I could live from that state of being even now as an adult. I realized I was not living that way. I lived in a prosperous country, where people talked about freedom. But was the freedom in our lives real and true? I questioned my life and observed other people's lives and I realized that in the rush of living, I had forgotten the true meaning of life, of one's true freedom; the feeling of a childlike happy heart.

I realized my life is in my hands, and not in the hands of society. It always had been, I had just forgotten that truth. I realized it is a powerful wisdom to own again. It takes courage to live the heart's truth, without following others' ideas and opinions. With this realization, I feel I no longer give my power away. In that moment, I knew—I am never alone and I can ask for guidance in any given situation. I returned to my true Self. I found the place of freedom and fearlessness within me again, out of the box, knowing that I am the Creator of my life and fully responsible, that no one other than me is responsible for anything in my life.

Everyone can only give advice from their point of view. I highly value people's advice and opinions, but nothing feels better and more accurate than my own answers. The answers that come from my authentic self have the greatest value for me. These answers feel right, positive and uplifting.

The heart is a safe place to meet with the Creator. IT is there for us through life until our last breath. I believe when we truly recognize that creative power within us, not only on a mental level but experiential level, there is no place for fear or insecurity. We feel the presence of that creative, absolute power of love, and that is freedom. It feels like being a child, not afraid of what tomorrow will bring. Eager to get up in the morning and create, and to experience new things, places with excitement. Living from the heart allows us to know that whatever we go through in life—there is a Higher Power taking care of us. Our work is to ask for guidance, to trust, to be thankful and to allow the flow of life.

My prayer is, "My Heart, please show me the way and I will follow." And I do. I allow myself to be silent every day to listen to my inner voice. I ask for guidance to show me my next step. The more I ask, listen, follow and live with an attitude of gratitude, the more guidance I receive. I choose to remember what I forgot in the busy-ness of the physical world. It was not enough for me to believe in God, I sought experience. It is the experience that makes a difference—remembering the greatness of our authentic heart. We are here to be different and to learn to be okay with it.

When I think back now, I understand what changed. I started thinking outside the box of a normal life. I started thinking about a new and more fulfilled life. I recognized what I always felt deep within, but never fully paid attention to the truth that I am physical and non-physical. The non-physical part of me creates through my body and IT always guides me to the best.

My new approach to life led me to new experiences. I started taking painting classes, making jewelry with semiprecious stones and crystals. I trained to become a yoga teacher, and I journaled. I did not do this to become perfect in anything. I did it to explore life. I wanted to do something new, just for the sake of joy, for myself, to feed my Soul, and do so without self-judgment. The way kids do it. I wanted to break through the boredom of normal life. I knew there was something beautiful in the simplicity of the pure joy I felt with everyday life, in the experiences where there was no competition, no need to be on-time, no thinking of survival.

Listening to people, I noticed how much our society is programmed to use words like should, could, would, can't, won't, have to. I believe life can be easier and brighter if we stop using these words. I believe there are many beautiful experiences waiting for us if we only have the courage to try something new, and let go of the same old patterns and beliefs we have gathered from other people and society.

Now I organize my time better. I make time to try new things. I let go of many old limited beliefs. Instead, I choose to believe that we have limitless potential, that we are unique and free to live our dreams, and free to create a life full of new experiences. It works. When I changed my beliefs, my reality changed. Our thoughts are powerful seeds.

Now, besides my job, I enjoy teaching yoga and meditation, making jewelry and painting. My passion is writing this book. I envision that this book will reach many people and will open the journey to a new life for them. For those who feel there is more to life than what they are living now.

With love to the Creator, my Higher Self, and all my Guides who are inspiring me.

Wisdom

- *You are the Creator, the Master of your Truth.*

- *Take your life in your hands and create a masterpiece.*

- *We create with our thoughts and visions.*

- *It is never too late to choose to live your dreams.*

- *You can only dream what you are capable of creating and living.*

- *Have the courage to try something new, something you always wanted to do but never have.*

- *You were born gifted, but your gifts only have value when you share them with the world.*

- *Be willing to let go of the old, which no longer serves you, and invite the new that brings you joy.*

Monday, June 18, 2012 - 9:48 am

Thoughts

Our thoughts are like seeds, they are complete packages of miracles. We can choose what we want to plant. If we plant thoughts of love, peace and joy, that is what will grow for us to harvest in life. If we focus on thoughts of fear, this will grow instead.

Thoughts are powerful magnets. Nothing in life happens by chance, or coincidence. Everything is by choice—conscious or unconscious. Thoughts always become things. It is the simple truth.

Wisdom

- *Plant the seeds of love, peace and joy and you will experience a life of bliss.*

- *Be grateful for your blessings and you will see them multiply.*

- *Be proud of who you are and thankful for your gifts.*

Tuesday, June 19, 2012 – 7:47 pm

Sunset at Coronation Park and Feelings of Gratitude

I am sitting here on the shore of Lake Ontario in Oakville's Coronation Park. It is a lovely evening after a hot day. The summer solstice is at the door with a new moon. I love coming here to sit and observe the waves washing onto the shore. It is peaceful here, especially in the evening when there are not many people around. It is quiet; a beautiful deep orange sun is setting and shining through the trees. I am reflecting on my day. I give thanks for all the gifts I receive today and every day. I am thankful for my health, for who I am, and for everyone in my life. I am thankful for the gift of writing, because this way I can share my best self, my essence with the world. I feel as though my hand writes without me thinking of what to write; I am simply the observer.

I feel this new chapter in my life is on the horizon. When we choose to live authentically, our lives change. My life changed when I reconnected with the Divine Light within me. When I started listening to my intuition, my Higher Self, the world of higher understanding opened for me. And I know it is waiting to be seen by all.

We are all here to share the wisdom of life, to grow together into an understanding of Oneness. We are approaching a new era on this planet. Our consciousness is rapidly changing. It is essential to take responsibility for our own life, our well-being and peace within. To trust the process is the key. We came here to experience this evolutionary change on a personal, global, and Universal level.

Sunday, June 24, 2012 - 6:30 pm

Many Lives

I am enjoying a summer Sunday afternoon. I see birds flying, some perennials already in full bloom and some ready to bloom. I enjoy this peaceful, warm afternoon with the blue sky and white flowing clouds that look like they are playing with each other. As I observe my surroundings and the beauty of the present moment, I listen to my inner voice and I feel deep peace. This voice talks to me when I feel relaxed; it gives me ideas, hints, and messages. Many times I do not know what they mean. I ask for clarity and I trust the process. Answers sometimes come unexpectedly, but it always feels peaceful, uplifting and inspiring.

I close my eyes and I see a big ship in my mind's eye. The water is calm, crystal-clear, and the ship moves slowly. It is a beautiful large sailboat, with its navy blue and white silky sails, and it is heading towards me. I see myself on the shore, but I look different than I do now. I am waiting for the ship to dock. The woman I see is wearing a navy blue dress, a white hat with a bow, lace gloves, and matching navy high-heeled shoes. I remember I had a pair of shoes like those in my early twenties, and I loved them. They were my favorite pair. I see this like a movie playing in my mind. I am smiling, happy to see the ship. Then, I see the woman change into a girl, perhaps ten years old. She is wearing a white dress, white shoes, and a white hat with pink flowers. I realize it is the early twentieth century.

I feel the breeze around my face and the vision ends.

I breathe deeply, and I am back in the present moment. I reflect on what I just saw. Somehow everything makes sense. It feels like me. I do not analyze it; I just want to feel it. I know everything happens for a reason and I do not need to know why this happened. I am back here in the moment observing my garden. I am inspired to write. I take my diary and I write down my experience.

I close my eyes and take a deep breath, and the woman in the navy dress pops into my mind's eye again. It looks as though the ship finally came to the shore. The woman seems to be happy. The ship makes a celebratory sound, and this pretty, slim, well-dressed woman is welcomed aboard. She likes to be there. She feels at peace there. She feels at home, blessed and strong. All is well, she knows. It never was otherwise. Maybe she forgot for a while that all is well.

Love is always in our heart, she realizes when she walks onto the ship. The ship is her Soul, which she reconnects with. Her Soul is a bright Light, holding many experiences through which comes the wisdom. Our wisdom is needed in our world today. It is why she decides to incarnate again, to have experiences to learn and grow, and to share the wisdom of her soul. She knows it is her purpose to be here.

I open my eyes. I feel this is a unique time to live again on planet Earth. I am on a path of self-discovery. I feel I know only a small part of my true self but I am willing to discover who I am on a deeper level. Writing is a powerful tool for self-discovery, a path of fulfillment for me.

I close my eyes and take another deep breath of the warm air and I listen to the outside world. I feel as though I am two hundred years in the past, hearing dogs in the distance and the sound of leaves rustling on the trees. It feels peaceful and, momentarily, I see myself on the porch of an old house writing a book that was never finished. I could not finish that book. I was punished.

Now I am free to finish my book and I do it with passion and love. I do not fear being who I am in this life time.

Wisdom

- *Choose to be free, choose to be true to yourself.*

- *Only when we are true to ourselves can we be true to others.*

- *Believe in yourself and your greatness no matter what others believe about you.*

- *Although you are whole and complete, you are always expanding, through your experiences, to a higher level of completion.*

- *Everyone sees themselves in you; we are all mirrors to each other.*

- *We see in others who we are.*

- *You are blessed with wisdom. Share it.*

- *Your wisdom is the brightest Light you can shine on the world.*

- *Listen to your calls and follow them.*

- *Living your Soul's truth is the teaching.*

- *We teach by example.*

Wednesday, July 4, 2012 - 9:45am

Life is Simple

I believe life is simple when we allow the present moment to be as it is. I believe we do not need to study human nature from books. If we go within, in stillness, we can access our own wisdom; body intelligence. It is vast, without boundaries and without others' perceptions. That wisdom is deeply seated within our Soul; it is not the mind's knowledge or beliefs we may have picked up from the outside. That wisdom is the inner voice, which always guides us, and wants the best possible outcome in any given situation. It is pure, our own, and always feels right when we follow it.

Life is as simple or complicated as we make it. The law of nature has simple principles, working in the same way for all of us. It is based on energy attraction, like attracting like. When our energy field holds vibrations of unworthiness, we attract lack, drama, and conflict. When we hold vibrations of worth we attract abundance of everything: love, peace, and all our material needs are met. Energy never lies. We all have different perceptions; we may see the same situation with different eyes, but the energy behind it; however, is the same. For example if it is fifteen degrees outside, some people may find it cool while others find it warm, yet we are all experiencing the same temperature.

Sunday, July 8, 2012 - 11:08 am

Coronation Park and the Synchronicities of the Number 414

Lately I see the number 414 often, on clocks, license plates and other places. Today I received an email for an Angel Workshop at 4:14 pm. I recognized the synchronicity and searched the meaning of the number on the Internet. The meaning strongly resonated with me.

The message was: "You are being divinely and angelically guided. Pay attention to your thoughts, dreams and daydreams. The angels are assisting you with your life purpose and Soul mission. You are fully supported by angels, Archangels and Ascended Masters. Trust your angels to deliver all that you will need."

The next day I went to Coronation Park. I wanted to take my dog for a swim, but when I called him he did not come. Instead, he stared at me from the back of the garden, unmoving. He usually runs to me when I call him to go to the park. I heard my inner voice say, "Just go by yourself," so I got my writing book and I left. Driving to the park, it felt right to go by myself. I heard, "Angels want to talk through you." As I heard that, I passed a car parked on the street with the number 414 on the license plate. Synchronicities are everywhere; they are real and always there. Divine Intelligence speaks to us. It always does. Because I pay attention to it, I hear it often.

Once I sat down and opened my book, I asked my Angels what they wanted to write through me. My hand started writing, and this was the result: You have an important purpose on this planet. Trust and love, and share this message: Love everything you see around you. Appreciate the beauty of nature. Be grateful for every moment because each holds wisdom and beauty, and it will never come back again. Every present moment is a treasure for all of us. See the greatness and the vastness of Now and only Now. All you have is Now. In the Now, there is love. Love is power and wisdom. Love is everything. Share the love and wisdom now, with everyone in your life and with everyone you meet.

My hand stopped writing and I felt gratitude for this moment and this love I experienced. I sat on the shore observing the stillness of the pen in my hand and the beautiful blue water completely still in Lake Ontario. This present moment was everything I could ask for, so rich, pure and real.

With gratitude to my Angels, Guides, Nature, the Creator and my Higher Self for NOW and the guidance they provide.

Wisdom

- *Only kindness, goodness, and compassion can tear down the walls of separation.*

- *The longest journey in life is from mind to heart, and the journey is worth it.*

- *If you focus on what is, you create more of what is.*

- *Still your mind to create happiness, a healthy vibrant body, a calm, clear mind, and an open loving heart.*

- *Good and bad is a perception in our minds. Our Souls do not categorize good and bad. Our Souls see life as an exploration, an expanding experience. Not categorizing is the perception of the Soul.*

- *When we realize we are here to learn and expand, we will no longer live in a world of duality; we will live from our heart. Only then, can our life be balanced and joyful.*

Thursday, July 12, 2012 - 7:53 am

Morning Pages

This summer is absolutely amazing. Today, birds are welcoming a new morning, singing a happy song. I love listening to the birds.

I like to write in my journal in the morning. I write about my feelings, my dreams, and my experiences. I have read that we dream every night. Some dreams we remember, some we do not. Sometimes my dreams are vivid. I like writing them down, I believe there are messages in dreams. There are times when I have questioned something in my life and many times answers would come to me through my dreams, other times through automatic writing. It takes practice but it works.

Sitting with a straight spine, body relaxed, I focus on my breath. We are more receptive when we keep our spine straight. It works like an antenna. When I feel I am ready, I start to write everything that comes to me without stopping. Sometimes it does not make sense to my mind, but I continue to write at least three to four pages and eventually the answer comes. There were a few times when I first started with automatic writing where the answer would not come. I have benefitted in different ways from this type of writing though, because it allowed me to unload from my subconscious mind what no longer served me. Then I would find my answers after a day or two. When our mind is clear the answer always comes.

Writing is a great healing tool. When I feel strong emotions I allow them to surface, and then I observe and release them through my breath. When I observe and breathe through a strong emotion, it loses power. I learned if I do not deal with the emotion, but rather cover it up or push it away it will come back again, usually stronger than the first time. When I start to feel low vibrational emotions, such as fear, surfacing, I start writing and keep writing until the low vibrations leave my body. It is essential to recognize the fear-based emotions as they surface and to work with them from the beginning, before they gain too much power. We are living in a world where we need to work, organize; take care of families, homes...etc. We may feel there are times when it is not easy to keep up with life's challenges. I know in situations like this it is essential for me to pause, meditate, journal, and ask: "What is important for me right now? What am I learning through this situation, while experiencing this emotion?" The answer is always within me, when I ask it is always revealed. Sometimes it comes to me through the feeling that all is well and I do not need to know more details. The feeling of peace comes and that is my answer.

The most important thing in life is well-being. I learned that when I feel grounded, clear, healthy, and energetically strong, life is a joy and challenges are more easily faced and overcome.

Wisdom

- *We are never alone. We are always connected to our Higher Self and our Guides. Writing is one way to connect with the unseen world.*

- *Make your well-being your priority in life no matter how many responsibilities you have. Only then can you achieve all your goals, visions, and responsibilities with ease.*

- *When you go through challenges try automatic writing, you may be surprised what comes through to you, and how much it may help you.*

- *All you ever need to know is within your own heart. You can always tap into your own wisdom. Find your own way to do it.*

- *When you find the way to listen to your heart you will find a best friend, a teacher, and a healer.*

- *Taking care of yourself before anything is called Self-love. Be your best friend, nurture yourself and the whole world will reflect that back to you.*

Thursday, August 2, 2012 - 7:52 am

Full Moon Meditation

Yesterday's full moon meditation was magical. There were nine of us and we sat outside by the fire in the quiet warm evening, with the stars shining through the sky. As we sat down, I gazed at the people around me and I saw a circle of life. We were ready to meditate, to go within to experience and witness their essence in the present moment. Through meditation we give ourselves permission to experience our depth.

I close my eyes and follow my breath, my body relaxes, my mind slows and I become an observer. My awareness observes my breath, my feelings, and my thoughts. The more I meditate, the greater an observer I become.

Meditation is an opportunity to learn about ourselves. I now recognize the landscape of my mind; I know myself on a deeper level and with that experience comes wisdom. I see my filter system clearly: my patterns and beliefs. Our patterns and beliefs run our daily lives. Some beliefs serve me, while others—those I have picked up from others during my journey—do not. In meditation, I am able to recognize who I am and who I am not, allowing me to release what does not serve me.

It takes courage and willingness to look at your own mind's functions, to realize, recognize, and release what does not belong to you. We often call it our baggage, and sometimes we carry it for many years, even lifetimes.

I realized meditation is a helpful healing tool, and because of this it has become a part of my lifestyle. To me, meditation is like a shower for the mind. It is as important to cleanse our minds on a regular basis, as it is to cleanse our bodies. I am thankful for all the beautiful Souls who were present at last night's meditation.

Wisdom

- *Meditation is the journey to Self.*

- *Meditation is the precious time spent with Self.*

- *Through meditation you may recognize and live your truth.*

- *When you live your truth, you teach by example, and you transform people's lives, even those who are passing by and never know you.*

- *Close your eyes, take a deep breath, and feel the sensations of joy, of simply being alive.*

- *Ultimately you reach the point when you begin seeking The Truth. The moment you know IT is not out there but rather within, you will know nothing is missing in your life, and you will know there is no way back. You will know you are whole.*

- *There is no failure or success on the path of truth. There are infinite possibilities of experiences to help us to expand.*

- *Life is a class you can never fail. You can only become more of who you are.*

Tuesday, August 7, 2012 - 8:38 am

Intention

Intention is the key to doing and achieving anything. I believe when good intentions are behind our action our job is well done, and we are satisfied and rewarded.

This year, and the next few years, will be filled with many changes and many people may feel challenged by life. I feel 2012 is the year of change for humanity. It is time for us to see life from a higher perspective, to see the bigger picture. We are moving through a self-realization process. It is becoming increasingly clear to people that we are connected through our hearts' vibrations, that there is no separation, but rather unity. People are realizing there is much more to know about what it means to be a human being. They are noticing that what we think and say creates our reality and affects all of us.

What is important behind every action is intention. When we do anything only for personal gain there is separation. When we act from the heart and focus on being in service to others, then all humans benefit. Through the understanding of unity, strength and abundance follows.

Wisdom

- *My life is not about what I do, it is about who I am, because everything I do reflects who I am. Everything I do comes from my state of consciousness.*

- *Abundance is the ability to live your highest potential every given moment.*

- *I choose unconditional love as an intention behind every action.*

- *When we feel Oneness we see the other person is us.*

- *Oneness is peace, harmony, and bliss.*

- *In Oneness there is no separation.*

Saturday, August 11, 2012 - 8:38 am

Vibrations

Our Earth's vibrations are rising higher. We are part of the Earth and we are affected by it. We are always changing with the Earth.

This is the time when we need to live with open minds, educate ourselves and allow ourselves to go with the flow. We need to let go of old habits and patterns and welcome the new. Everything we look at, including our thoughts, is energy. It is in our best interest to allow these higher vibrations to do their job. It is part of the evolution of the Universe.

Choosing to go with the flow of life, we can help ourselves to raise our energy vibrations and the transformation could not be easier. There are many different ways to raise the vibrations of our body. Self-love is the most important. When we truly love ourselves we not only take care of our physical body, but we also see the importance of our inner self. For well-being and a healthy body it is important to eat healthy organic food that is free of chemicals, to drink pure water, to exercise, to relax and rest. For mental and spiritual well-being, we must be aware of what we feed our minds. Pay attention to what we listen to, read, watch, and where and with whom we spend time. Meditation or the quieting of the mind is important for receiving guidance in our life. When we love ourselves our body holds high vibrations and we do not resonate with anything that does not match our vibrations. We can only attract food, people and situations that are a vibrational match to us.

Out of Self-love comes worthiness and from that place we can make conscious choices for the best possible outcomes in our life. We know we hold high vibrations, because we value our life and our priority is to be true to ourselves and to be peaceful no matter what is going on around us. It is our responsibility to give of ourselves first. Only then we are able to share the love we feel in our heart with others. It is a false belief, an illusion to think that people or things can make us feel happy. Happiness must come from within.

It is empowering to know that we have the free will and the power to create the life we want if only we choose? If all of us realize that and take responsibility for our well-being and happiness we would create the world we want to live in. When we create expectations for our happiness or blame others for unhappiness, we are giving our power away and we are losing the strength to create what we hold in our vision. If we focus our power to create our dream, we can live our dream.

When I close my eyes, I see a world where we understand that each of us is a powerful co-creator. I see a world where people celebrate their existence, their uniqueness, and they share their gifts with passion and love. I see that we all understand and follow the Law of the Universe and we no longer need man-made laws. I see us celebrating the world we have been waiting for. It feels like a painter's vision. Artists always see the painting in their mind's eye and then start to transfer it to the canvas. Our planet Earth is the canvas and humanity is the painter. Now, more and more people are ready to paint on this canvas, ready to paint a picture together we call life.

Wednesday, August 22, 2012 - 4:44 pm

Mountains

I am amazed by the beauty of a field of colourful wild flowers surrounding me and this inspires me to write. Everything looks magical, the blue sky with cloud formations, the sun, and the moon.

My husband and I are spending the day at the Scandinavian Spa in Collingwood. Earlier this day, we booked a vacation in the Swiss Alps. As I gaze at the beautiful scenery around me, I feel like I am already in Switzerland. I have never been there in this lifetime, but I feel memories are coming back. We have a call to go there. Maybe that is why my husband had such a strong urge to book this vacation. It feels like we are going home, even though I was born in a different part of Europe.

In the spring, I went to an intuition workshop. During some of the exercises two participants saw big mountains in their minds as they were focusing on my energy field. We did not know each other and, at that time, I was not planning this vacation. I was surprised when they told me about the mountains, and I asked myself what this could possibly mean.

Sitting here, at the Spa I close my eyes and I see a beautiful country with mountains. The memory of being strongly connected to Europe, our homeland, where we lived many lifetimes, is coming back.

Attila and I know we were together before and we know we had to be together again in this life. While we are in the Alps, we will celebrate our wedding anniversary. I feel those mountains represent our love, our strength, and the beauty of our relationship. Mountains, just as life, have peaks and valleys. There are ups and downs. One cannot exist without the other. When sharing true love, nothing is impossible. We go through the mountains of life together. We understand and support each other. We enjoy the view from the top of the mountains and the heat of the sun's rays. When we come down to the valley we may not have the same view, but we walk through the valley and make the best of our journey, even when we cannot see the sun. We may not see as much as we do from the top, but we know we are free to rise to the top again and enjoy the view.

Life is like that. We have a freedom of choice. It is always up to us where we want to be in life, in the valley or on top of the mountains. Life has value no matter where we are. We are always part of a whole, experiencing and learning something new.

Thank you, Creator, for the inspiration. I see love in everyone and everything.

Wisdom

- *We are here to create and celebrate relationships with meaning.*

- *Unconditional love is the foundation of lasting relationships.*

- *Cherish those who are not afraid to go with you through the mountains of life.*

- *The heart's connection makes the impossible, possible.*

- *If there is love there is no question. True love understands.*

- *Love within is what we need to tap into, to feel complete.*

- *Embrace the essence of who you are and share it with the world.*

- *Love is all that is.*

Friday, August 24, 2012 - 10:30 pm

Energy

While we sleep we connect with the Source. When we have a deep, restful sleep we feel relaxed and energized when we get up. The Source energy is high vibrational energy. It recharges our batteries. We need energy to speak, to see, to work, to create our day. Our free will allows us to choose how we spend our energy. It is important to create an awareness of where we invest the gift of Source energy.

Posing myself questions helps me stay aware of myself, of my surroundings, of my feelings. I ask myself: "Where do I invest my energy? Do I use my energy to create a life that benefits me and all?" These questions help me to see where my intentions lie, and where my energy flows.

Everything in life is energy. Our life situations and the people around us reflect our energy fields back to us. Nothing is a coincidence, even though we may choose to call it so. Everything in life is a vibrational match to our energy field. If we want to change anything in our life we need to start within. We need to focus on changing our own vibrations to be able to experience change outside of us.

Taking the responsibility for our own energy field is required. The attitude of gratitude, healthy food, exercise, good sleep, meditation—just to name a few—will help keep our energy balanced.

Wisdom

- *What we send out comes back.*

- *What we see in others exists in us. Do not judge others and you will not be judged.*

- *Radiate love and love will come back to you.*

- *Feel and listen to your energy field, it will always tell you the truth.*

- *Self-love expands your energy field.*

- *The Universal Law of Attraction works on an energetic level.*

Sunday, September 23, 2012 – 5:23 pm

Déjà Vu and Synchronicity

My husband and I are planning a vacation to different places in Europe. We plan to stay in Switzerland, but I have a call to visit the cathedral in Milan, Italy—Domm de Milan. We will also visit Attila's daughter in Strasbourg, France. We want a hotel close to the old city, so we can explore the architecture. Searching online, I picked three small, nicely updated hotels because we prefer simplicity and comfort. I could not make a decision on which to book. I asked the Spirit to give me a sign.

A day later, I held a meditation circle in my yoga studio at home. It was a small class: me, two other women, and a man. As we sat down to meditate, the man said, "It's nice to be here, in this small circle with three beautiful roses." Hearing his words, I thanked the Spirit for my answer on which hotel to book. We booked the Three Roses hotel the next day.

Strasbourg felt like home, such a lovely place to visit. I was happy my husband could visit his daughter and her family. The nearby hotel was great, our small room cozy and clean. All we needed for a few nights. We visited with his daughter, and then we went out for a walk along the river in the beautiful old town. Later that night we returned to our hotel room, as I was taking off my jeans and sweater I experienced a déjà vu moment... I had a vision of myself unzipping a red and black satin dress with black lace on the skirt. An image came to my awareness that I was removing black gloves and a hat. Then I saw myself place my clothes on a wooden stand in the corner. In the room there were two big windows with heavy curtains, and in my mind's eye they were changing to lacy cream curtains from the heavy orange curtains currently in the room. To my surprise I had stepped into a previous life's energy. It was the beginning of the nineteenth century. I knew I had a good life there, because feelings of comfort and beauty flooded me. I was aware of walking into this room that I had tapped into a past life, but the present moment was the most important reality. This experience felt very real to me. I observed my experience, and then I let it go. The smell of roses from that nineteenth century room surrounded me, as I drifted off to sleep.

Wisdom

- *In life there are no coincidences just coexisting incidents. Everything happens for a reason.*

- *There are synchronicities showing us the lives we've lived and will live, and energetically, they happen simultaneously with the life we are currently living.*

- *Pay attention to synchronicities, déjà vus, and signs, this is the Spirit language talking to your Soul.*

- *Ask for signs and stay in tune, I believe there is a reason we experience past memories.*

Monday, September 24, 2012 – 2:22 pm

Mountain Meditation

I am sitting here with my husband on top of the Champery Mountains in the beautiful Swiss Alps. My face touched by the sun and a light breeze. Everywhere I look I see mountains standing tall. I close my eyes and I feel the mountains within me. I feel oneness with everything around me. I feel the sun, the earth, the blue sky and clouds dancing around the sun. I feel the grass and small stones against my hands as I touch Mother Earth. It is a magnificent nature. I feel the snow on the mountaintops in the distance. I hear the rain—from the past. Yes, it rained this morning and everything looks fresh and green. I can feel how the rain nurtures the nature surrounding me.

Deeper into my feelings, I feel the colour emerald green expand in my heart. I feel and hear the wisdom of the mountain. I hear my inner voice whispering, "Always stay tall, stay calm and magnificent in every season, like we, the Mountains, do. Sun, rain, wind, snow, we are the same, beautiful, standing tall."

I open my eyes, and feel shivers all over my body. Everything looks even more beautiful. I am absorbing this amazing message of truth with every cell of my body. I breathe deeply and feel the whole Earth within myself. In stillness I realize it takes little time to go back to my true Self, back to my heart, to feel the oneness with the Creator and with nature.

I turn to my husband, ours eyes meet in the silence of this present moment, and we feel the beauty of nature within. There is no need for words, as words cannot describe this moment. It is the experience that speaks. We value these precious moments we spend together. We know only this moment and the love is real.

Wisdom

- *When you are continuously active, there is no time to acknowledge the truth of your life purpose and to be aware of your true Self.*

- *In stillness you access your truth, potential, wisdom, purpose, and oneness with Creator.*

- *Stillness is your loving home; you always find love, peace and balance there.*

Saturday, November 24, 2012 - 6:30 am

Wisdom Messages from My Higher Self

The coloured leaves of fall are covering the ground. I am sitting by the fireplace looking through the window, feeling cozy as I get ready for my morning meditation. I embrace these quiet times where I meet my Soul, where I tap into my inner space, wisdom, and guidance within. This is the place where unconditional love lives. Where there is no limitation or fear. Where there is the power of the Creator. It is being home.

Sometimes I ask my Soul questions before I meditate. Today, I have no questions. I feel a certain clarity and knowingness; I will close my eyes and feel the softness of my breath. After meditation, I will journal my experience.

This is what came through me today...

The only way you can feel fulfilled is to have faith and trust in Divine Light, to believe in your Higher Self even though you can neither see nor touch it. You can, however, hear it when you quiet your mind. This inner voice is easier to hear when in stillness. When we trust ourselves and detach from our mind, we are choosing to be in the present moment. Then, when we let go of the need to know the outcome we are able to see life as a miracle.

When you feel lost in your life you start searching for love. Not outside of you but within. Love within is the power that will take you through any challenge in your life. Change is a choice. Trying does not make things happen. So, do not try—do. Make a choice and change will follow.

Are you acting on your highest joy? When you do you are living your truth every given moment.

Saturday, November 24, 2012 - 5:55 pm

Dream Big

My inner voice says, "Dream big," and this is not the first time. A numerologist friend of mine told me the same thing as my inner voice. In fact, I have heard it from people upon first meeting them.

These signs have been obvious. How could I not pay attention to these two words? So I asked myself what it means to dream big. What could I possibly dream big? I closed my eyes and listened to my heart. In my mind's eye I saw many people reaching to me for guidance and I was happy to be with them and thankful for their trust. My intention is to share my gifts with those who are ready to live their truth, their potential, and their dreams.

I teach small yoga classes, meditations, and workshops and I am thankful for all my gifts and all the people who come to me and trust me. I sense there are many more people I will be reaching, perhaps with this book.

When I sit in stillness information is revealed to me.

For thousands of years we were conditioned to listen to the outside world and to follow. I feel now is the time for all of us to step out of the box, take our power back and start listening to our own voice. That voice is the wisdom we earned through our life, and many other lives. Within us is a library that we can access called the Akashic Record.

My inner voice continues whispering, "Dream Big." I close my eyes, turn my focus within and ask myself, "What is my big dream?" My mind shows me physical objects. It feels good, but it does not fulfill my heart. My feelings are bigger and my dreams are much greater than physical things. So this morning when the Spirit asked me to write about my big dream, I wrote this:

My Big Dream is to reach millions of readers. To tell them that all of us here on our planet we call Earth can dream big and live our dreams. We are vast spiritual beings, living in physical bodies with unlimited potential. Our planet is rich, and the Creator within us already knows how to fulfill our dreams. Our work is to have vision and faith. Our dreams are within reach. Dear Reader: "DREAM BIG."

Thanks to my Higher Self and to my Guides. May our dreams come true.

Wisdom

- *We only dream what our Soul is capable of creating.*

- *We are here to create a joyful life.*

- *We are here to help each other through serving each other.*

- *We are here to realize that we are extensions of ONE GOD.*

Sunday, November 25, 2012 - 11:23 pm

Coming Back to Myself Through Being a Seeker

All my life, I have been a seeker of truth. At a very young age I felt I was different from other kids. It was not easy for me, and not easy for those around me. When my siblings were watching cartoons I was bored; I kept looking for something creative and fun to do. I was unsure of what I sought; however, I had a deep feeling inside that there was more in life to explore.

In my teenage years I loved to go to the small bookstores in town. The books that interested me were books about ancient civilizations, or history of the earth, books about nature, and herbs.

In the late eighties my sister brought me a book about natural healing—an eastern approach, discussing meridians and chakras, how our body, mind and Soul are connected—when I was in the refugee camp in Austria, I treasured that book. It was written in my mother's language, and in English the title would translate to Puzzle of Life. Reading it then, I did not clearly understand what it was about, but I do remember it resonating with me, and I went back to that book over, and over, again for more clarity.

It took me years to realize that I was seeking, the truth of who I am and how the human body works. I sought what they did not teach me in school—that being human is more than the physical body. Later in my life, I realized that all the information I sought was in my heart. The books I found and liked to read were just reminders.

When I came to Canada my life challenges—learning to adapt to a new environment, a new culture, learning a new language, looking for a job—were different from my life back home. I never lost my faith and always believed in truth. I believed in a higher power, guiding me on my life journey. I felt deep within me that all is well no matter what my life experience was.

I believed that we continued existing after death even though many people I knew did not believe that, and it was sometimes a challenge for me to interact with them. I did not know how to put my feelings—what I could not see or touch—into words.

I never changed my beliefs about my deep knowing. I must say, I adopted many beliefs from others, which I released later in my life. However, no one could take the belief away from me that we are Infinite and there is much more to life than the physical plane. I could not explain it. I did not have the vocabulary. I simply knew. There were not many people to talk to about it anyway. At least, I did not know them. Sometimes I felt unfortunate, like an outsider.

In my early forties, I started attracting open minded people, people who believed we are also unphysical. I know I had changed, and that was the reason I attracted these people. I was not the only believer and I became more selective. I changed my diet, stopped drinking alcohol, carefully chose the places I would go, and who I spent time with. I stopped listening to and watching the news. I took yoga classes and meditation. At times it was challenging, but I was willing to clean up my body and my life and become me again.

I have read books about ancient wisdom, meditation, yoga, the Mayan calendar, energy healing, the earth and human evolution, Egypt's pyramids, astrology, and numerology. I have gained knowledge on a variety of topics through YouTube videos. I have listened to other people's opinions and observed them. I kept for myself what resonated and let go of what did not. I joined many different groups out of curiosity so I could hear what people were experiencing on their journeys. I went to meditation retreats and I experienced many different healing modalities with different healers. I wanted to have my own experiences.

For me it was not enough just to read or hear about what I wanted to know.

After years of reading, studying, practicing yoga, going to workshops, and doing my own research, I found the truth I was looking for. It had been inside of me all along. I found it through silence. Reading books gave me knowledge. Being in silence gave me the experience of my inner wisdom. There was no book or healer who could give me the same experience. I realized all the books and healers were tools and the key was to use the tools.

The answers to all my questions lived within me. All the creative energy and inspiration—was in me. The healer, the guidance, the ultimate truth I sought—all within me.

I realized the truth of freedom, meaning that I can be who I want to be, regardless of outside approval and that everything in my life is a reflection of who I am. My only job is to act upon my highest joy and everything else will fall into place. I found that there is no right or wrong. Everything in life is experience. I became an observer of life. I realized that life is much easier when we stop putting labels on everything.

Now I understand that each of us holds our own truth and that all of us have a unique destiny to complete. Every book I have read, every workshop I have attended and every person I have interacted with, has taken me forward to meet my own Self, my Truth. Every step I've taken in my life has happened to bring me back into my true self, where there is love, peace, silence, playfulness, creativity, freedom, and wisdom; where I am unlimited, infinite, and beautiful.

Wisdom

- *Beauty comes from within.*

- *I sought answers outside until I realized all I seek is within.*

- *There is no better teacher, healer, and knower than the one within your own heart.*

- *Trust your inner voice and you will be rewarded.*

- *Your Soul loves you most.*

- *You are the only knower of your truth.*

- *You live your truth, when you follow your heart and feel blissful.*

- *"Acting upon my highest joy is my priority," is a good mantra to lead your life.*

Wednesday, November 28, 2012 – 3:33 pm

Big Things Come Easy

It is a cold November afternoon and light snow covers the ground. Winter is approaching, but I feel warm and cozy in my house. Wood is burning in the wood stove. I breathe in the fresh scent of Eucalyptus essential oil evaporating from a ceramic bowl sitting on top of the stove. I sit down to meditate, embraced in the feeling of deep stillness, listening to the voice of my Soul, and I hear, "Go and write." I ask the Spirit what to write about and I hear, "Big things come easy."

As I listen to the Spirit voice within me, one of the teachers who crossed my path came to my awareness. He always said, "You don't have to go and get it, just be and receive." Even though deep inside I believed life was about easiness and simplicity, my mind refused to believe it. I knew life was supposed to be effortless and joyful. Still, my mind questioned how I could just be and receive. I wanted to have my own experiences and I thought I needed to create them. I asked the Spirit to show me how to do this.

My awareness expanded as I took a deep breath and closed my eyes. I began to see the unconscious beliefs I had picked up on my life's path. Many of us are often exposed to narrow minded perceptions from others. Things like: no pain, no gain; or, you have to work hard and long hours to achieve a good life. It became clear to me that I possessed a deep knowing of how to live a simple and easy life even though my mind still held on to the belief that hard work was necessary to survive. Though I did manifest work I liked and beautiful things for which I am thankful, after many years living with these beliefs, and working hard, I realized it was not the way to live. I became aware that if I want to be fulfilled in my life I needed to look closely at my limited beliefs and release them. I learned to trust my deep knowing that a joyful life can be simple and effortless.

Thursday, November 29, 2012 - 9:15 am

Seeking Answers

I was guided to go to the park to connect with Nature, so I went to Coronation Park in Oakville. I sat on the shore, staring at the water and asked the Spirit, "Why is it that the harder I try to do anything, the more unfulfilled I feel?" I again heard the teacher's words, "Just be and receive." Hmm, that's the answer.

As I am sitting and observing my surroundings and the beat of my heart, I felt at peace. I felt clarity and the connection to my heart. All I heard was, "Be and receive."

Observing the surface of the calm and clear blue water, I heard a soft voice whispering, "Nothing is more important in life than being true to Self... your feelings, your well-being and doing what interests you most at every given moment." It sounded strong and empowering. I heard it over and over again as I sat there... It felt like a mantra. The inner voice continued. When you do so everything in life comes to you effortlessly. Listen to your intuition. You will be guided what to do, where to go and you will feel fulfilled.

My life was changing because I was willing to change my beliefs. I was willing to listen to my Soul's wisdom in the silence, its voice soft and loving, yet powerful.

I often hear, "Take your diary and write about your feelings and experiences," so I do and it always makes me feel more myself. My mind surrenders and my Soul expands. In my heart, I feel home, satisfied, fulfilled, in total opposition to when I push myself hard to accomplish something. Doing this gave me more time for my hobby, which, surprisingly, brought me income too. It also gave me more time to write this book. As I create and observe my life, I understand what my teacher meant by be and receive. I know when we make ourselves a priority and we stay relaxed, when we ask for guidance, and act on it, life is much easier. This is how we create a meaningful life.

Being and receiving means to act upon the highest joy. From this state we can live with ease because we allow ourselves to be moved by the energy that rotates our planet. That is the energy of our powerful creator.

Thanks to all my teachers, physical and nonphysical, to my guides, my Higher Self and to the Creator.

Wisdom

- *When we put ourselves first and we feel good, we attract good things in our life.*

- *I feel good because I am alive, I do not need any other reason.*

- *Receive the gift of the present moment as that is all we have.*

- *Letting go of beliefs which did not serve me made me see who I am.*

Monday, December 3, 2012 - 6:40 pm

The Purpose of Life

We all have this question at some point in our life, "What is my purpose, my mission in my life?"

All of us are born with special gifts and talents. We can clearly see these gifts in our young children. They all have different interests and those are their gifts and talents. When we allow them to be who they are born to be, support their interests, and do not control them, they will grow-up with strong self-confidence, ready to walk their life's path with purpose.

Some children are artistic, they like to paint and work with their hands. Others like mathematics or science. Some like to read and write, or build things. And there are children that love animals and nature. Deep inside we know we have a mission to complete.

Once I visited a friend who was a schoolteacher and there hung a beautiful painting in her living room. When I first saw it, shivers raced down my spine because of the love for art that was evident in every stroke. I asked her where she got the painting and she told me one of her twelve-year-old students had painted it. I responded, "She is a born artist." That sentence came out of me without thinking. My friend then told me the child's parents wanted her to go to law school as her father was a lawyer. I said nothing, but silently questioned why the parents did not see and support their daughter's gift. This made me wonder why parents project their needs onto their children rather than seeing the gifts and talents they possess, their life's purpose.

I silently sent love to these parents and the artistic girl, praying for her to be strong and to find her way to her truth. I know from my own life that many times we make choices out of love for our parents. We take roads they want us to take, but when we stay strong, the roads we choose not to walk on lead us to find our own.

With Love and Blessings to all parents.

Wisdom

- *Living what we do not want helps us realize it is in our best interest to choose what we want.*

- *Your purpose, your mission is one of a kind. It is your dream and a gift to humanity when you live it.*

- *To awaken your true life's purpose you have to be willing to allow change. It may come in the form of change of consciousness, change in beliefs, thought patterns, and a change in lifestyle choices.*

- *Allow the change to live your life purpose.*

Wednesday, December 19, 2012 - 9:22 pm

Angels Are Always With Me

I just finished a session with a client and I am reflecting on my experience. For years, during my hairdressing career, clients gave me gifts for Christmas. I realized a few years ago that those gifts had deeper meaning. Many of those gifts were angel ornaments or cards with pictures of angels. One of my clients gifted me with a table runner that had angels on it. I have crystal angels, wooden angels, an angel lamp, and chimes with the words angels gather here. One client gave me a card and told me that when she saw it she thought of me.

I have loved everything about angels since I was a child. The word angel sounds soft and loving to me. When I close my eyes and think of an angel, I see a beautiful body floating in a light pink, green, blue, and white soft dress. They are always balanced and flowing with easiness. I feel protection and purity when I think of angels.

My mother had stitched a beautiful picture that hung over my bed when I was a child. It had two children crossing a bridge with an angel in a pink dress watching over them. I remember looking at that picture and always feeling love for that angel. I always believed in Angels and a Higher Power.

Everything is energy. When we vibrate at the frequency of the angelic realm, we feel a connection to them, to their presence, and to their guidance.

As I write this, strong shivers move across my body, especially around my head. For me this is the sign the angelic realm is present.

This morning my client of many years brought me a gift, homemade cookies she makes for me every year. She always creates a beautiful package. Today she put her cookies in a tin with three angels painted on the lid. As she gave me this gift of love, I noticed one of the angels pressing its hands to its heart and the word, believe. My body filled with feelings of warmth and I heard believe in yourself, you can write this book. As I turned over that tin, I noticed the other angel and the words joy and peace. I heard the words…it will bring you much joy and peace. It feels right to express my creative self. I feel I have done what I was guided to do by my Angels.

Wisdom

- Angels, Higher Self, Guides are always watching over us, always waiting for us to ask them for help.

- To stay aware is important if we want to hear the messages.

- When we ask Angels to answer our questions, and we follow the guidance, we will feel fulfillment that will bring us joy and peace.

- Our heart—Soul knows better than our mind.

Saturday, January 12, 2013 – 7:17 pm

Deep Wisdom

I woke up this morning feeling appreciation for a new day. Lying in my warm bed with my eyes closed, I listen to the stillness, the peace in the bedroom, and in my heart. I hear the words: deep wisdom, deep wisdom, I hear it repeated as I focus on the softness of my breath.

I open my eyes, look through the window, and see it is a cloudy, snowy day; a perfect day to sit by the fireplace and write a chapter in my book. More words whisper in my mind, "Write about deep wisdom." I am inspired.

After a few deep breaths my hand moves, writing of its own accord.

In every heart there is a deep wisdom, a knowingness of truth. We are more than we think we are. Words are not enough to describe the depth of the heart's wisdom. The heart is a library, a keeper of everything. In our hearts we know what to do, where to go. In our hearts we hold the depth of eternal true Love. Our heart holds these gifts.

Wisdom or knowingness is different from knowledge. Wisdom comes from the experience of many lifetimes, from the feelings we have lived. It comes from the heart, it is ours, and no one can ever take it away from us. It is our treasure forever. Knowledge is from the mind, what we learn through life from parents, teachers, society, and books, each other. Knowledge is other people's ideas and can be valuable and useful for us. However, until we access and trust the wisdom of our Soul we may not feel fulfillment in life. We may be seeking more, because our heart is always with us reminding us that there is expansion. Consciousness is always expanding.

The heart is the seat of the Soul, the place of wisdom, the place of unconditional love and Oneness. It is the first organ that is created in the mother's womb, and from the heart everything else grows into a beautiful human being. The heart knows that being human is a miracle, that we are extensions of Source, of Creation.

My hand stopped.

I am thankful to the wisdom of my Soul.

Wednesday, February 13, 2013 - 2:31 am

Do Not Give Up

I woke early this morning and could not get back to sleep. My inner voice whispered, "Go write." I did not pay attention to the whisper, turned around, and tried to sleep. I didn't feel like leaving the warmth of my bed. I wanted more sleep, but was unsuccessful. Fully awake, I felt the creative energy move through me. I heard the voice again, "Go write, never give up." Hmm, never give up. The words wouldn't let me sleep. Never give up. The voice was soft, but strong.

I made myself to get up, I drank a glass of water and grabbed my notebook. I did not want to use my computer, and although I was wide awake my eyes wanted rest. I turned on a lamp for light, and took a couple of deep breaths as the action always helped to get me started. My body relaxed, and I was glad to be sitting there, ready to write. I listened and let the writing be spontaneous. I wrote what I heard, making the automatic writing easy, whereby I relax and let it happen.

As I focused inward and listened, I traveled back to my early twenties, before my emigration, to a song I listened to a lot back then by a popular German duo called Modern Talking. They had many good songs, mostly in English, but I had my favourite and listened to it when I was home alone.

I now realize I listened to that particular song as I worked through some challenges. Singing whatever words I picked up as I did not understand English then, but I always felt better afterward, with a renewed ability to keep moving through my challenging life. I had a young daughter, a full-time job, a plan to emigrate, and big dreams. Preparing to emigrate, I knew I had to keep up and stay strong. I had a call.

After I had immigrated to Canada, my sister sent me a Modern Talking CD. She remembered how I always liked their music. When I saw the

CD, my memory immediately returned to the eighties, back home. The song I replayed was Don't Give Up. At the time, I did not know the meaning of the lyrics, not one word. But it kept me going... As I listened to it again, understanding the lyrics, it all made sense. I understand now that everything is energy; every word, thought, or song has energy vibrations, even if we do not understand the language. I believe that energy kept me going. At the time, I needed to hear it, to feel the music. Those song lyrics spoke to me on a vibrational level encouraging me not to give up.

Our energy field, our body intelligence understands the energy of sound. We always attract what we need.

As I continued writing, I took a few deep breaths, recognizing—again—how creative and gifted human beings are and that everything around us in the Universe is expansive. Everything is energy. Our thoughts and emotions are vibrating energy frequencies. We were energy before we came into our bodies, and we will remain energy after we leave our physical bodies. Our true essence can't die. Energy always exists, it only changes form. It is empowering to remember this truth, the truth that we are much more than we realize; we are infinite.

In life, it is essential to keep up, never give up, and to remember our vibrational self. We have a destiny to complete. We each have our own call. Each of us is an equally important piece of the puzzle creating the whole picture. The picture can't be complete without the importance of each of us.

As I sit here, finishing this chapter of my book, I am sending unconditional love to every human heart. I wish for everyone to stay strong and to not give up.

Wisdom

- *You are meant to live your dreams.*

- *We were born to thrive, when we live our dreams we thrive.*

- *What we focus on we create more of.*

- *Giving up is not believing in yourself.*

Saturday, February 16, 2013 – 3:45 pm

The Animal Spirit and Unconditional Love

Sometimes we do not know why things happen until later on. My daughter had wanted a dog. When she was fifteen we decided to get her a dog. Interesting, to observe the synchronicities—I got my dog, Rexo, for my fifteenth birthday.

We wanted to surprise Daniela with a puppy, so we said we were going for a country drive. When we stopped at a farm, Daniela was puzzled and then we told her that we were there to pick a puppy. She was surprised and excited.

When we approached the house, the puppies ran towards us. There were four left in the litter for us to choose from. The smallest one ran to me and chewed on my shoelaces. This was funny because I was the one least interested in getting a dog. Yet he ran straight to me. Daniela decided to take him and said it was because he had picked me.

We sat in the car with this cute German shepherd puppy and we named him Rexi. Little Rexi cried on the way to his new home. I knew it was natural because we had been taken him from his mother. As I listened to Daniela comforting him, I realized my heart was totally open to loving this little dog. How could I not?

It was the end of July when Rexi started his journey with us. We had so much fun with him. He was a very loving dog. He loved the outdoors and his freedom. Running around our backyard was his favourite pastime. He was always where we were, curious and well-behaved.

We took him up north, when we rented cottages or went camping. He was great with people, especially children. When Daniela left for university I spent more time with him. I realized dogs could only share unconditional love. It did not matter to him how I felt, he always ran to me with excitement. Observing him I learned so much. He was always happy, always in the present moment, always sharing his best self. He grew into a beautiful, healthy dog with a loving personality.

When Rexi was eight years old Daniela brought home a kitten. We were hoping they would get along since Rexi was a big dog and not used to having another pet around. After a few days, they were good buddies. Playing and sleeping together on one big pillow. When Rexi was ten, Daniela finished university and moved into her own home. She got a golden retriever puppy. Later on he came to our home, his name was Lopci but we called him Lopi. They were great together, the two dogs and a cat we called Cici.

When Rexi was fourteen and a half his time to leave us had come. I never wanted to experience his passing. I could not imagine myself present at his last breath. I loved him—for his greatness and unconditional love—it was hard for me to think about it. It was early November and a light rain fell when it happened. I was the only one home with him. He passed naturally, outside in our garden, where he loved to run and play with his furry friends Cici and Lopi. I stayed with him, holding him, and praying for his easy passing. When he passed I cried and Lopi brought me Rexi's toy. I covered Rexi with a blanket and waited for my husband to come home.

It was an unforgettable experience. I was touched to be there with him, to be there for him. Only I know how many times Rexi was there for me. He picked me the first day we met, as my daughter said. And he picked me to be there on his last day, too.

Sometimes things happen in life, they have a deep meaning that we only realize later on.

Rexi showed me the meaning of pure unconditional love and he also proved to me I do not have to fear death. It was definitely a beautiful, meaningful experience. Praying for life to end with easiness. Memories returned. I felt all those beautiful moments, we, as a family, spent with Rexi. I will always have fond memories of our times up north, jumping on the trampoline with him, and going for walks. I was thankful, I felt love and appreciation for the animal kingdom, for the day-to-day routines with our pets we sometimes take for granted. I will never forget him. He deeply shaped my Soul. I am thankful.

Recently, a friend told me about an animal communicator in BC. My curiosity to connect with Rexi in the Spirit world—through her—was strong. I had felt his presence before. I contacted her through e-mail and she sent me the most profound and accurate message. I was stunned. Rexi never died for me, he simply let go of his old body, although, he still looked handsome at the end of his life.

Sunday, May 5, 2013 - 9:54 pm

Women Who Showed Me Their True Selves

When I came to Canada, I did not speak any English. I understood some words but I had a hard time communicating. I never liked TV, but I wanted to hear the English language and hoped watching English programming would help me learn.

Going through many TV channels, I found I liked to watch Oprah. I had no idea what they were talking about for a long time but I liked her voice, her smile, how she presented herself. I liked her ability to listen and I could feel her intention was to help people. Her show was the only show that resonated with me. Later on, when I began to understand English, I enjoyed her shows even more and I learned that she understands people's life challenges because she went through her own. I see her material success as a reflection of her unconditional love for others. I see that what she does, she does with passion. To me, Oprah is sharing her true self with humanity and that makes her well known all over the globe.

Dear Oprah, Thank you for being one of my inspirations, one of my heroes. Watching your shows, I saw your understanding of the human heart. With your presence you hold a loving space for millions, to help them on their journey to happiness and freedom. And you always share your joy when people celebrate theirs. Be blessed for your greatness and love.

Growing up, I loved Tina Turner's songs and sang them in my own way, which was not in English. I mimicked the sounds the best I could, as I did not speak English. Every time I heard Tina I felt happy, uplifted. Many times, unable to resist, I danced just for fun.

In my eyes, the whole world looked more beautiful when I heard Tina's singing on the radio. I knew little about her, I had seen only pictures in magazines. Information during the seventies was limited in my country. When I immigrated to Austria in the late eighties, Tina had a new song called Simply the Best, and for the first time I saw her video on television. I saw a woman of strength. I witnessed Tina share her passion for what she did, and her true self, with her fans. She did what she loved and shared her happiness, always smiling.

After a few years of living in Canada, I saw the movie about Tina Turner's life and the challenges she had faced. After finding out Tina's early life experience was so extreme; I admired her even more, for her strength, her faith in God, and herself. I wanted to know more about her, so I started reading about her. I found out she was born the same year as my mom and this made me feel closer to her. I felt like she was a good friend of many years, even though I had never met her.

I wished to see her one day. When Tina came to Toronto, my family and I went to her concert. It was one week before my birthday. What a great gift.

Tina is an amazing woman in my eyes. In her eyes, I see passion for life and how she loves to see people happy at her performance. She is strong and soft at the same time with a beautiful feminine energy. Tina, thank you for being who you are.

Dear Tina, You are simply the best. You have been an idol to me since childhood. Love to you and best wishes.

Around 2000, I moved through a transformation in my life. I knew deep inside that I needed to make changes in my life. To live my dreams fully I had to let go of beliefs that were not truly mine and to let go of the baggage I carried. I knew there was much more to life than what I was living. I searched for the missing puzzle pieces.

I always believed in Creator, in God, in an unseen force. How could Earth possibly turn without IT? I wanted to know and to experience more of my truth, without conditions. I asked—Who am I? Why am I here? What are my gifts? How can I serve humanity?

Constantly questioning myself, a book ended up in my hands. A client that had carried it to our appointment, and lent it to me. It was Louise Hay's—*You Can Heal Your Life*.

The book changed my life. My eyes opened, and many other doors for knowing the true wisdom of my heart opened too. I found Louise on YouTube and listened to her words of wisdom and many other writers and speakers from Hay House. Her life story and her story about how this book was born fascinated me. I see Louise's willingness to help people, to understand who they are. It comes from her heart and from her life experiences. To me that is a powerful teaching.

I see Louise's trust and belief in the greatness of life. With this attitude she is teaching by example. I admire Louise, now in her eighties, because she still helps people on their paths with her simplicity, purity, and devotion to serve others with the gifts of her heart.

Dear Louise, I am thankful our paths crossed through your great book. You inspired me to teach by example. I wish you the very best.

What I see and admire in the wonderful Souls of Oprah, Tina, and Louise is that, although they walked challenging paths, they never gave up. Instead, they openly shared their strength, learned through their experiences, and moved on. They share the wisdom they have gained. It is clear to me they love what they do and through sharing their gifts with love and passion they inspire many people to do the same. I believe we are all gifted in different ways and when we share our gifts we serve humanity. When we do what we love, life is much easier, effortless, meaningful and beautiful. I call it living in bliss. What I see is their intention to inspire people, to feel good and to live their dreams. This is why they have such devoted fans. I believe many of us want to feel fulfilled and live our dreams. And I also believe it is the birth right of every human being to thrive. We come here to experience duality so we know how it feels and we can choose what we want—what feels best for us.

I believe there is no need to be a victim. I believe we all experience life's episodes as victims on different levels, but these experiences are there for us to grow and to overcome and shine our Light. It is our choice to live wisely. It is what I see in Oprah, Tina, and Louise and many other women I know in my life.

My wish is to meet all three of you one day. Your life stories and your service to humanity inspire me.

Friday, May 10, 2013 – 7:47 pm

Why Do You Want To Be a Teacher?

I am guided to write again. I heard an echo in my head, "Why do you want to be a teacher?" A yoga teacher asked this question of me. He asked that we write an essay about it as part of our coursework.

When I first heard the question, I thought: I do not want to be a teacher, I just want to know the teachings, the science behind the ancient wisdom of yoga—for myself—because my husband and I attended yoga classes and we liked it. Always curious about new things, new ways, I wanted to know more.

The question sat for a few days, as I did not know what to write. I tried to figure it out, but struggled with what I could possibly write about. Thinking back, I cannot remember what I filled three pages with. The only sentence I remember clearly, with a strong feeling of my true self, is: If I ever become a teacher, I know I want to teach by example. It resonated with me.

I strongly believe teaching by example is the only way. When we are true to ourselves we are holding space for others to become true to themselves.

Friday, May 17, 2013 - 10:22 pm

Thanks to My Husband

I want to thank you, Attila, for the unconditional love you have shared with me through the years we have been together. We have walked our journey side by side for the last twenty-five years and I want to tell you, your love is like God's love.

God's Love.
God loves us unconditionally.
God lets us be who we are.
God lets us make mistakes through which we evolve.
God lets us make choices for ourselves.
God lets us experience constructive and destructive paths.
God always stays by our side.
God is always there for us.
God never leaves our heart.
God always forgives us.
God is unconditional love itself.
I see the God within your heart.

Your love is like God's love. I love you for being who you are. You taught me how to love unconditionally. You are the teacher in my life. Without you I would not be the person I am today. At your side, I learned to be my true self. You are the mirror of my Light and my shadows. I now see the world through the eyes of love. Your love is forever in my heart.

Be blessed on your life's journey, Attila, and never forget the greatness of your heart.

I love You.

Thursday, September 26, 2013 – 6:36 pm

Looking Back and Being Thankful

Today is twenty-five years since I crossed the border into Austria with my daughter and my husband (we were not married at the time). That was the day we started our journey together. My life plays like a movie in my mind. I see clearly why certain things happened as they did. They shaped me into who I am.

I feel how I live my life today is a reward for not giving up, for getting up every time I fell down, and for trusting in the goodwill of life, and in my dreams. I have a great husband and an amazing daughter who is now carrying her first child, my first grandchild. There are no words to describe this miracle of life I am experiencing. The feeling of becoming a grandmother in three months is a deep feeling of gratitude in my heart.

I close my eyes and I feel the softness and warmth of Daniela's skin when she was born thirty years ago. I feel her little hand in my hand when I first walked her to school in the small Austrian town of Gusswerk. I feel her silky hair as I combed it. I hear her laughter as she played with the other kids. I feel her happiness when she dressed-up in flowery dresses for school. She always loved bright flowery dresses.

I remember how much she wanted a dog when she finished elementary school. How excited and loving her eyes were when we surprised her with Rexi. I see her responsible nature when she learned to drive a car. I see her grown up when she bought her first car to commute to University. The day of her graduation was my forty-fourth birthday, and this milestone in her life was a great gift. I see a beautiful woman, standing tall in her navy blue graduation gown holding her sociology degree, her silky brown hair and loving eyes looking out at the crowd as she stands on the stage with her fellow students and friends. It is a gift from God to have the blessing of a beautiful, wise, loving, caring woman I am proud to call my daughter. I did the best I knew. I am thankful to God for this blessing. I am thankful to God I met Daniela's father. I know he is proud of her too. Back home in Europe he has his own family, a wife, son, and daughter. I am happy for us. Happy we found our own ways. The wounds of our past are healed. They are forgiven. We see in children what love creates. Everything was part of the Divine plan.

I remember the warm summer day, a few years ago when Daniela introduced her boyfriend, Jean-Philippe, to us. That evening after they left, my husband and I knew they were in love. We felt that JP would become her husband.

I am happy for them. When I see Daniela now, growing into a mother, happy to have her own family, I am thankful for this gift in my life. I watch how all my blessings in life grow and multiply like branches on a tree. The fruits of life are delicious.

I remember Daniela surprising me with a visit. When she is in the area, she often pops in. I love when she just shows up at the door and we have a cup of tea together. She stretched her body on the sofa and put her feet up for few minutes and drifted away. I sat beside her and put my hand on her baby belly, and felt the baby move. I felt love beneath my hand. Looking at Daniela's beautiful, innocent face, she looked like a girl herself. I used to watch her sleep and sometimes captured those moments in pictures. Watching her sleep, feeling the precious baby move inside her, I am amazed with God's gifts. I am thankful.

I never thought observing Daniela sleeping when she was a little girl would be so deeply coded in my heart years later. I watched her playing, eating, sleeping, laughing, studying because I was enjoying the moment. Now I know I had been collecting treasures into my heart's treasure box. I love seeing her belly grow and seeing her and JP create their cozy home. He is already a great father, creating a connection by talking to their baby in Daniela's belly. They chose not to discover the sex of the baby, wanting to be surprised at the birth. We will know just before

Christmas. I am grateful for the most precious gift God is giving me for Christmas this year—Life, a grandchild.

I love you my first precious grandchild. I am looking forward to meeting you soon. I feel like I already know you. All of us know you are a very special gift to our family. Love to you and to your amazing parents.

Wednesday, October 23, 2013 – 7:04 am

Married for 24 Years

I woke up this morning, opened my eyes and saw a cloudy day through the window. I felt good and warm in bed on this cool October day. I watched my husband peacefully sleeping. His dark hair against the white pillow put a smile on my face.

I closed my eyes, tightly covered myself with our duvet to feel the last few minutes before we started our working day. I felt my husband's deep Soul residing in his heart. Our wedding anniversary is next week. We were meant to be together. I know we were together before and we did not complete our journey then. That was the reason we met again. There was a strong attraction between us when we first met. Nothing is a coincidence in life. We met in this lifetime to complete our journey.

I reflect back to our beginning, both of us felt like we knew each other and we wanted to be together. It was a strong knowing. Then, we did not know what we know now.

We came to our marriage with beliefs we had picked up along our path before we met, unresolved emotions, fears…past lives. Sometimes life was a challenge, but we learned from each other. Love for each other and willingness to be our best gave us strength to overcome many challenges. Being together, we learned who we are and who we are not. I would not want to change anything about my past with Attila. I see every day of our marriage was and is a gift and an opportunity to make our relationship shine stronger.

In our life together we are teachers and students at the same time. We do the best we can. We share our Light and our shadows with each other. It is a blessing that we are together. No one knows me better than Attila. I am thankful for knowing his pure heart and his earthly shadows. Knowing the whole and loving unconditionally makes people shine. We believe in our dreams, we trust and now we celebrate again, as we do every year. We have grown out of buying each other many presents. We have everything we need. The greatest gift for me is the time we spend together. This year we are going to the theater. And Attila always buys me a beautiful bouquet of flowers. It always reminds me of our wedding day in the Austrian Alps when I was a bride marrying a man whose love will always stay in my heart.

We understand life takes different turns; these turns are unseen to us in the present moment. We know whatever is there for us on our journey, is there for us to grow. The love we shared until now is forever, and that is what I cherish.

I am thankful for the gift of unconditional love in our relationship.

Thursday, November 7, 2013 - 2:20 pm

Prayer for Gabriel

I am thankful for this warm November day. I walked by the lake at Coronation Park in Oakville, where I like to take my dog, Lopci. He was playful and loving as always.

I paused and sat down for a moment. My book came to my awareness. I wrote a big part of my book here, nature inspired me to write. I am so happy the writing for my book is completed. My friend, Kelly—the editor—is working on it. We met over a year ago, but it feels like I have known her much longer. People are showing-up on my path, helping me with the completion of this book. I am grateful for each of them. I believe this book will encourage many people to live authentically, to believe in themselves and to love themselves. And that is my intention and wish for this book.

I looked up to the clear, blue sky, feeling the vastness of the universe and warmth of this beautiful day and I offered my prayer. I thanked Archangel Gabriel for help with the completion of my book. I sent blessings and gratitude to Kelly for the great work in editing.

I love to offer my simple prayers of gratitude through the day. They give me strength to move forward.

As I looked down from the sky, I observed my dog playing with a stick. I noticed a boy, around eight years old, coming towards me. He wanted to play with Lopci and I was happy to see them having fun. I surrendered to the moment. Life is meaningful when we live aligned with the moment. When we stop wanting something other than what is. When we allow life to unfold.

I turned to this happy, little boy and I asked him his name. He said, "My name is Gabriel," Oh, I was stunned. I said out loud, "Thank you, God. Thank you, Gabriel."

Monday, December 23, 2013 - 11:48 pm

Words For My Loved Ones

Dear Felix, I've been waiting for your birth to complete this book. I dedicate this book to your mother, but this last chapter is for you, my first dear grandchild.

Your mother is my amazing daughter, she showed me great love and I know she is sharing that love with you too. Your dad is a great man, I watched him talk to you before you were born. We all had great fun guessing whether you would be a boy or a girl while your mom carried you. Your parents believed they were having a boy.

There is so much I want to share with you. One day I will tell you all about the special day when you were born. This Christmas will be one to remember for all of us.

The night you were born was cold and cloudy, but magical. We arrived at the hospital before eight o'clock in the evening where your parents patiently awaited your birth. Your mom was in pain and your dad was comforting her. I silently prayed for your mom, and for you to arrive soon and safely. All of us were ready to welcome you with love.

The room was cozy and your parents were happy and ready to see you. It was after midnight when the doctor said you would come soon. In the early morning your mom released a sound of joy and I heard your first cry. I squeezed my hands together and I thanked God.

When you arrived, Felix, I felt so much joy and love coming from the room, merging with the love I felt in my heart. It was the moment I will never forget.

All of us were very happy to see you for the first time, our happy, lucky Felix. It was a precious moment when your mom gave you to me to hold.

I am grateful and I know how much joy and fun you are going to share with the whole family.

Tonight your dedko (grandfather) and I took Lopci for a walk. The night was peaceful with bright stars were shining in the clear sky. There had been freezing rain and everything sparkled with ice and looked magical. You were born right after the winter solstice as the sun shines more directly on the earth. Like the sun, you brought more light into the world. The world feels beautiful and bright having you here with us, Felix, we love you—unconditionally—forever. Welcome to our family.

~~~~~~

My dear daughter Daniela, now we are not only women but also mothers. I know we are always the best mothers we can be. I wish your son shares joy and love with you, as you have with me. Being by your side as you gave birth to my first grandchild, I felt the pain of your labor and the deep joy and love of you giving birth to a new life—your son.

~~~~~~

Dear JP, you are the son I never had. Your big loving heart makes you a great dad. I am looking forward to seeing you grow into a proud father.

~~~~~~

My beloved husband, Attila: thank you from the depth of my heart for sharing the responsibility of raising my daughter, Daniela.

I love you ALL. We are ONE.

ONLY LOVE.

Dear Reader,

If you ever thought to write a book about your life, or you have another heart's call, I encourage you to do it. Follow the call. Never underestimate your gifts and talents. They may not feel real in the beginning, but don't give up, trust yourself and follow your heart's call. Follow your bliss. Believe in yourself and in your dreams.

Remember your essence is UNCONDITIONAL LOVE. You are worthy otherwise you would not exist. God does not make mistakes. Every mind's imperfection is Divine perfection.

I believe you attracted this book for a reason and I believe it delivered a message that would serve you in some way on your life's journey. It is my wish to you.

This work is truly my own. My life. My words. My emotions. It was a true learning experience for someone whose English is a second language. Always interested in trying new things in life, I decided writing this book would be a good exploration. Having enjoyed the experience I feel that I will continue to write.

Blessings,

Daniela

www.ingramcontent.com/pod-product-compliance
Lightning Source LLC
LaVergne TN
LVHW051728080426
835511LV00018B/2939